THIS BOOK BELONGS TO:

_____

_____

Pizza Tasting Journal

DATE _____   PIZZERIA _____

NEIGHBOURHOOD _____

BEVERAGE PAIRING _____

TOPPINGS

- ☐ CHEESE
- ☐ MUSHROOMS
- ☐ GREEN PEPPER
- ☐ OTHER ....

- ☐ ONIONS
- ☐ BACON
- ☐ SAUSAGE

- ☐ PINEAPPLE
- ☐ TUNA
- ☐ BLACK OLIVES

CHEESE

- ☐ GREASY
- ☐ STINGY

- ☐ SMOKEY
- ☐ STINKY

- ☐ CREAMY
- ☐ SALTY

SAUCE

- ☐ SWEET
- ☐ TANGY

- ☐ THIN
- ☐ SAVORY

- ☐ SPICY
- ☐ CHUNKY

FRESHNESS ① ② ③ ④ ⑤   CRUST ① ② ③ ④ ⑤

CRUST

- ☐ BUTTERY
- ☐ CRISPY

- ☐ SPONGY
- ☐ BUBBLY

- ☐ CHEWY
- ☐ OTHER............

NOTES

....
....
....

WOULD YOU TRY AGAIN?
- ☐ YES   ☐ NO

OVERALL RATING
★ ★ ★ ★ ★

Pizza Tasting Journal

DATE _____ PIZZERIA _____

NEIGHBOURHOOD _____

BEVERAGE PAIRING _____

TOPPINGS

☐ CHEESE ☐ ONIONS ☐ PINEAPPLE
☐ MUSHROOMS ☐ BACON ☐ TUNA
☐ GREEN PEPPER ☐ SAUSAGE ☐ BLACK OLIVES
☐ OTHER ....

CHEESE

☐ GREASY ☐ SMOKEY ☐ CREAMY
☐ STINGY ☐ STINKY ☐ SALTY

SAUCE

☐ SWEET ☐ THIN ☐ SPICY
☐ TANGY ☐ SAVORY ☐ CHUNKY

FRESHNESS ① ② ③ ④ ⑤   CRUST ① ② ③ ④ ⑤

CRUST

☐ BUTTERY ☐ SPONGY ☐ CHEWY
☐ CRISPY ☐ BUBBLY ☐ OTHER...........

NOTES

....
....
....

WOULD YOU TRY AGAIN?   **OVERALL RATING**

☐ YES   ☐ NO   ☆ ☆ ☆ ☆ ☆

Pizza Tasting Journal

DATE _____ PIZZERIA _____

NEIGHBOURHOOD _____

BEVERAGE PAIRING _____

TOPPINGS

- ☐ CHEESE
- ☐ MUSHROOMS
- ☐ GREEN PEPPER
- ☐ OTHER ....
- ☐ ONIONS
- ☐ BACON
- ☐ SAUSAGE
- ☐ PINEAPPLE
- ☐ TUNA
- ☐ BLACK OLIVES

CHEESE

- ☐ GREASY
- ☐ STINGY
- ☐ SMOKEY
- ☐ STINKY
- ☐ CREAMY
- ☐ SALTY

SAUCE

- ☐ SWEET
- ☐ TANGY
- ☐ THIN
- ☐ SAVORY
- ☐ SPICY
- ☐ CHUNKY

FRESHNESS ① ② ③ ④ ⑤   CRUST ① ② ③ ④ ⑤

CRUST

- ☐ BUTTERY
- ☐ CRISPY
- ☐ SPONGY
- ☐ BUBBLY
- ☐ CHEWY
- ☐ OTHER...........

NOTES

....
....
....

WOULD YOU TRY AGAIN?
☐ YES   ☐ NO

OVERALL RATING
★ ★ ★ ★ ★

Pizza Tasting Journal

DATE _____ PIZZERIA _____

NEIGHBOURHOOD _____

BEVERAGE PAIRING _____

TOPPINGS

- ☐ CHEESE
- ☐ MUSHROOMS
- ☐ GREEN PEPPER
- ☐ OTHER ....

- ☐ ONIONS
- ☐ BACON
- ☐ SAUSAGE

- ☐ PINEAPPLE
- ☐ TUNA
- ☐ BLACK OLIVES

CHEESE

- ☐ GREASY
- ☐ STINGY

- ☐ SMOKEY
- ☐ STINKY

- ☐ CREAMY
- ☐ SALTY

SAUCE

- ☐ SWEET
- ☐ TANGY

- ☐ THIN
- ☐ SAVORY

- ☐ SPICY
- ☐ CHUNKY

FRESHNESS ① ② ③ ④ ⑤   CRUST ① ② ③ ④ ⑤

CRUST

- ☐ BUTTERY
- ☐ CRISPY

- ☐ SPONGY
- ☐ BUBBLY

- ☐ CHEWY
- ☐ OTHER...........

NOTES

....
....
....

WOULD YOU TRY AGAIN?

☐ YES   ☐ NO

OVERALL RATING

★ ★ ★ ★ ★

Pizza Tasting Journal

DATE _____   PIZZERIA _____

NEIGHBOURHOOD _____

BEVERAGE PAIRING _____

TOPPINGS

- ☐ CHEESE
- ☐ MUSHROOMS
- ☐ GREEN PEPPER
- ☐ OTHER ....

- ☐ ONIONS
- ☐ BACON
- ☐ SAUSAGE

- ☐ PINEAPPLE
- ☐ TUNA
- ☐ BLACK OLIVES

CHEESE

- ☐ GREASY
- ☐ STINGY

- ☐ SMOKEY
- ☐ STINKY

- ☐ CREAMY
- ☐ SALTY

SAUCE

- ☐ SWEET
- ☐ TANGY

- ☐ THIN
- ☐ SAVORY

- ☐ SPICY
- ☐ CHUNKY

FRESHNESS ① ② ③ ④ ⑤   CRUST ① ② ③ ④ ⑤

CRUST

- ☐ BUTTERY
- ☐ CRISPY

- ☐ SPONGY
- ☐ BUBBLY

- ☐ CHEWY
- ☐ OTHER............

NOTES

....
....
....

WOULD YOU TRY AGAIN?
- ☐ YES   ☐ NO

OVERALL RATING
★ ★ ★ ★ ★

Pizza Tasting Journal

DATE

PIZZERIA

NEIGHBOURHOOD

BEVERAGE PAIRING

TOPPINGS

- ☐ CHEESE
- ☐ MUSHROOMS
- ☐ GREEN PEPPER
- ☐ OTHER ....

- ☐ ONIONS
- ☐ BACON
- ☐ SAUSAGE

- ☐ PINEAPPLE
- ☐ TUNA
- ☐ BLACK OLIVES

CHEESE

- ☐ GREASY
- ☐ STINGY

- ☐ SMOKEY
- ☐ STINKY

- ☐ CREAMY
- ☐ SALTY

SAUCE

- ☐ SWEET
- ☐ TANGY

- ☐ THIN
- ☐ SAVORY

- ☐ SPICY
- ☐ CHUNKY

FRESHNESS ① ② ③ ④ ⑤   CRUST ① ② ③ ④ ⑤

CRUST

- ☐ BUTTERY
- ☐ CRISPY

- ☐ SPONGY
- ☐ BUBBLY

- ☐ CHEWY
- ☐ OTHER...........

NOTES

....
....
....

WOULD YOU TRY AGAIN?

☐ YES   ☐ NO

OVERALL RATING

★ ★ ★ ★ ★

Pizza Tasting Journal

DATE _____ PIZZERIA _____

NEIGHBOURHOOD _____

BEVERAGE PAIRING _____

TOPPINGS

- ☐ CHEESE
- ☐ MUSHROOMS
- ☐ GREEN PEPPER
- ☐ OTHER ....
- ☐ ONIONS
- ☐ BACON
- ☐ SAUSAGE
- ☐ PINEAPPLE
- ☐ TUNA
- ☐ BLACK OLIVES

CHEESE

- ☐ GREASY
- ☐ STINGY
- ☐ SMOKEY
- ☐ STINKY
- ☐ CREAMY
- ☐ SALTY

SAUCE

- ☐ SWEET
- ☐ TANGY
- ☐ THIN
- ☐ SAVORY
- ☐ SPICY
- ☐ CHUNKY

FRESHNESS ① ② ③ ④ ⑤   CRUST ① ② ③ ④ ⑤

CRUST

- ☐ BUTTERY
- ☐ CRISPY
- ☐ SPONGY
- ☐ BUBBLY
- ☐ CHEWY
- ☐ OTHER...........

NOTES

....
....
....

WOULD YOU TRY AGAIN?
☐ YES   ☐ NO

OVERALL RATING
★ ★ ★ ★ ★

Pizza Tasting Journal

DATE _____ PIZZERIA _____

NEIGHBOURHOOD _____

BEVERAGE PAIRING _____

TOPPINGS

- ☐ CHEESE
- ☐ MUSHROOMS
- ☐ GREEN PEPPER
- ☐ OTHER ....

- ☐ ONIONS
- ☐ BACON
- ☐ SAUSAGE

- ☐ PINEAPPLE
- ☐ TUNA
- ☐ BLACK OLIVES

CHEESE

- ☐ GREASY
- ☐ STINGY

- ☐ SMOKEY
- ☐ STINKY

- ☐ CREAMY
- ☐ SALTY

SAUCE

- ☐ SWEET
- ☐ TANGY

- ☐ THIN
- ☐ SAVORY

- ☐ SPICY
- ☐ CHUNKY

FRESHNESS ① ② ③ ④ ⑤   CRUST ① ② ③ ④ ⑤

CRUST

- ☐ BUTTERY
- ☐ CRISPY

- ☐ SPONGY
- ☐ BUBBLY

- ☐ CHEWY
- ☐ OTHER...........

NOTES

....
....
....

WOULD YOU TRY AGAIN?

☐ YES   ☐ NO

OVERALL RATING

☆ ☆ ☆ ☆ ☆

Pizza Tasting Journal

DATE _____   PIZZERIA _____

NEIGHBOURHOOD _____

BEVERAGE PAIRING _____

TOPPINGS

- [ ] CHEESE
- [ ] MUSHROOMS
- [ ] GREEN PEPPER
- [ ] OTHER ....

- [ ] ONIONS
- [ ] BACON
- [ ] SAUSAGE

- [ ] PINEAPPLE
- [ ] TUNA
- [ ] BLACK OLIVES

CHEESE

- [ ] GREASY
- [ ] STINGY

- [ ] SMOKEY
- [ ] STINKY

- [ ] CREAMY
- [ ] SALTY

SAUCE

- [ ] SWEET
- [ ] TANGY

- [ ] THIN
- [ ] SAVORY

- [ ] SPICY
- [ ] CHUNKY

FRESHNESS ① ② ③ ④ ⑤   CRUST ① ② ③ ④ ⑤

CRUST

- [ ] BUTTERY
- [ ] CRISPY

- [ ] SPONGY
- [ ] BUBBLY

- [ ] CHEWY
- [ ] OTHER...........

NOTES

....
....
....

WOULD YOU TRY AGAIN?

- [ ] YES
- [ ] NO

OVERALL RATING

⭐ ⭐ ⭐ ⭐ ⭐

Pizza Tasting Journal

DATE _____ PIZZERIA _____

NEIGHBOURHOOD _____

BEVERAGE PAIRING _____

TOPPINGS

- [ ] CHEESE
- [ ] MUSHROOMS
- [ ] GREEN PEPPER
- [ ] OTHER ....

- [ ] ONIONS
- [ ] BACON
- [ ] SAUSAGE

- [ ] PINEAPPLE
- [ ] TUNA
- [ ] BLACK OLIVES

CHEESE

- [ ] GREASY
- [ ] STINGY

- [ ] SMOKEY
- [ ] STINKY

- [ ] CREAMY
- [ ] SALTY

SAUCE

- [ ] SWEET
- [ ] TANGY

- [ ] THIN
- [ ] SAVORY

- [ ] SPICY
- [ ] CHUNKY

FRESHNESS ① ② ③ ④ ⑤   CRUST ① ② ③ ④ ⑤

CRUST

- [ ] BUTTERY
- [ ] CRISPY

- [ ] SPONGY
- [ ] BUBBLY

- [ ] CHEWY
- [ ] OTHER...........

NOTES

....
....
....

WOULD YOU TRY AGAIN?

- [ ] YES
- [ ] NO

OVERALL RATING

☆ ☆ ☆ ☆ ☆

Pizza Tasting Journal

DATE _____ PIZZERIA _____

NEIGHBOURHOOD _____

BEVERAGE PAIRING _____

TOPPINGS

- ☐ CHEESE
- ☐ MUSHROOMS
- ☐ GREEN PEPPER
- ☐ OTHER ....

- ☐ ONIONS
- ☐ BACON
- ☐ SAUSAGE

- ☐ PINEAPPLE
- ☐ TUNA
- ☐ BLACK OLIVES

CHEESE

- ☐ GREASY
- ☐ STINGY

- ☐ SMOKEY
- ☐ STINKY

- ☐ CREAMY
- ☐ SALTY

SAUCE

- ☐ SWEET
- ☐ TANGY

- ☐ THIN
- ☐ SAVORY

- ☐ SPICY
- ☐ CHUNKY

FRESHNESS ① ② ③ ④ ⑤   CRUST ① ② ③ ④ ⑤

CRUST

- ☐ BUTTERY
- ☐ CRISPY

- ☐ SPONGY
- ☐ BUBBLY

- ☐ CHEWY
- ☐ OTHER...........

NOTES

....

....

....

WOULD YOU TRY AGAIN?

☐ YES   ☐ NO

OVERALL RATING

★ ★ ★ ★ ★

Pizza Tasting Journal

DATE _____ PIZZERIA _____

NEIGHBOURHOOD _____

BEVERAGE PAIRING _____

TOPPINGS

☐ CHEESE ☐ ONIONS ☐ PINEAPPLE
☐ MUSHROOMS ☐ BACON ☐ TUNA
☐ GREEN PEPPER ☐ SAUSAGE ☐ BLACK OLIVES
☐ OTHER ....

CHEESE

☐ GREASY ☐ SMOKEY ☐ CREAMY
☐ STINGY ☐ STINKY ☐ SALTY

SAUCE

☐ SWEET ☐ THIN ☐ SPICY
☐ TANGY ☐ SAVORY ☐ CHUNKY

FRESHNESS ① ② ③ ④ ⑤   CRUST ① ② ③ ④ ⑤

CRUST

☐ BUTTERY ☐ SPONGY ☐ CHEWY
☐ CRISPY ☐ BUBBLY ☐ OTHER...........

NOTES

....
....
....

WOULD YOU TRY AGAIN?   **OVERALL RATING**

☐ YES ☐ NO   ☆ ☆ ☆ ☆ ☆

Pizza Tasting Journal

DATE _____   PIZZERIA _____

NEIGHBOURHOOD _____

BEVERAGE PAIRING _____

TOPPINGS

- ☐ CHEESE
- ☐ MUSHROOMS
- ☐ GREEN PEPPER
- ☐ OTHER ....
- ☐ ONIONS
- ☐ BACON
- ☐ SAUSAGE
- ☐ PINEAPPLE
- ☐ TUNA
- ☐ BLACK OLIVES

CHEESE

- ☐ GREASY
- ☐ STINGY
- ☐ SMOKEY
- ☐ STINKY
- ☐ CREAMY
- ☐ SALTY

SAUCE

- ☐ SWEET
- ☐ TANGY
- ☐ THIN
- ☐ SAVORY
- ☐ SPICY
- ☐ CHUNKY

FRESHNESS ① ② ③ ④ ⑤   CRUST ① ② ③ ④ ⑤

CRUST

- ☐ BUTTERY
- ☐ CRISPY
- ☐ SPONGY
- ☐ BUBBLY
- ☐ CHEWY
- ☐ OTHER...........

NOTES

....
....
....

WOULD YOU TRY AGAIN?
☐ YES   ☐ NO

OVERALL RATING
★ ★ ★ ★ ★

Pizza Tasting Journal

DATE ▢▢▢▢▢ PIZZERIA ▢▢▢▢▢

NEIGHBOURHOOD ▢▢▢▢▢

BEVERAGE PAIRING ▢▢▢▢▢

TOPPINGS

- ☐ CHEESE
- ☐ MUSHROOMS
- ☐ GREEN PEPPER
- ☐ OTHER ....

- ☐ ONIONS
- ☐ BACON
- ☐ SAUSAGE

- ☐ PINEAPPLE
- ☐ TUNA
- ☐ BLACK OLIVES

CHEESE

- ☐ GREASY
- ☐ STINGY

- ☐ SMOKEY
- ☐ STINKY

- ☐ CREAMY
- ☐ SALTY

SAUCE

- ☐ SWEET
- ☐ TANGY

- ☐ THIN
- ☐ SAVORY

- ☐ SPICY
- ☐ CHUNKY

FRESHNESS ① ② ③ ④ ⑤   CRUST ① ② ③ ④ ⑤

CRUST

- ☐ BUTTERY
- ☐ CRISPY

- ☐ SPONGY
- ☐ BUBBLY

- ☐ CHEWY
- ☐ OTHER...........

NOTES

....
....
....

WOULD YOU TRY AGAIN?

☐ YES   ☐ NO

OVERALL RATING

★ ★ ★ ★ ★

Pizza Tasting Journal

DATE _____ PIZZERIA _____

NEIGHBOURHOOD _____

BEVERAGE PAIRING _____

TOPPINGS

☐ CHEESE ☐ ONIONS ☐ PINEAPPLE
☐ MUSHROOMS ☐ BACON ☐ TUNA
☐ GREEN PEPPER ☐ SAUSAGE ☐ BLACK OLIVES
☐ OTHER ....

CHEESE

☐ GREASY ☐ SMOKEY ☐ CREAMY
☐ STINGY ☐ STINKY ☐ SALTY

SAUCE

☐ SWEET ☐ THIN ☐ SPICY
☐ TANGY ☐ SAVORY ☐ CHUNKY

FRESHNESS ① ② ③ ④ ⑤   CRUST ① ② ③ ④ ⑤

CRUST

☐ BUTTERY ☐ SPONGY ☐ CHEWY
☐ CRISPY ☐ BUBBLY ☐ OTHER...........

NOTES

....
....
....

WOULD YOU TRY AGAIN?
☐ YES   ☐ NO

OVERALL RATING
★ ★ ★ ★ ★

Pizza Tasting Journal

DATE _____ PIZZERIA _____

NEIGHBOURHOOD _____

BEVERAGE PAIRING _____

TOPPINGS

- ☐ CHEESE
- ☐ MUSHROOMS
- ☐ GREEN PEPPER
- ☐ OTHER ....

- ☐ ONIONS
- ☐ BACON
- ☐ SAUSAGE

- ☐ PINEAPPLE
- ☐ TUNA
- ☐ BLACK OLIVES

CHEESE

- ☐ GREASY
- ☐ STINGY

- ☐ SMOKEY
- ☐ STINKY

- ☐ CREAMY
- ☐ SALTY

SAUCE

- ☐ SWEET
- ☐ TANGY

- ☐ THIN
- ☐ SAVORY

- ☐ SPICY
- ☐ CHUNKY

FRESHNESS ① ② ③ ④ ⑤   CRUST ① ② ③ ④ ⑤

CRUST

- ☐ BUTTERY
- ☐ CRISPY

- ☐ SPONGY
- ☐ BUBBLY

- ☐ CHEWY
- ☐ OTHER............

NOTES

....
....
....

WOULD YOU TRY AGAIN?
☐ YES   ☐ NO

OVERALL RATING
★ ★ ★ ★ ★

Pizza Tasting Journal

DATE **_____** PIZZERIA **_____**

NEIGHBOURHOOD **_____**

BEVERAGE PAIRING **_____**

TOPPINGS

- ☐ CHEESE
- ☐ MUSHROOMS
- ☐ GREEN PEPPER
- ☐ OTHER ....
- ☐ ONIONS
- ☐ BACON
- ☐ SAUSAGE
- ☐ PINEAPPLE
- ☐ TUNA
- ☐ BLACK OLIVES

CHEESE

- ☐ GREASY
- ☐ STINGY
- ☐ SMOKEY
- ☐ STINKY
- ☐ CREAMY
- ☐ SALTY

SAUCE

- ☐ SWEET
- ☐ TANGY
- ☐ THIN
- ☐ SAVORY
- ☐ SPICY
- ☐ CHUNKY

FRESHNESS ① ② ③ ④ ⑤   CRUST ① ② ③ ④ ⑤

CRUST

- ☐ BUTTERY
- ☐ CRISPY
- ☐ SPONGY
- ☐ BUBBLY
- ☐ CHEWY
- ☐ OTHER...........

NOTES

....
....
....

WOULD YOU TRY AGAIN?

☐ YES   ☐ NO

OVERALL RATING

★ ★ ★ ★ ★

Pizza Tasting Journal

DATE _____ PIZZERIA _____

NEIGHBOURHOOD _____

BEVERAGE PAIRING _____

TOPPINGS

- ☐ CHEESE
- ☐ MUSHROOMS
- ☐ GREEN PEPPER
- ☐ ONIONS
- ☐ BACON
- ☐ SAUSAGE
- ☐ PINEAPPLE
- ☐ TUNA
- ☐ BLACK OLIVES
- ☐ OTHER ....

CHEESE

- ☐ GREASY
- ☐ STINGY
- ☐ SMOKEY
- ☐ STINKY
- ☐ CREAMY
- ☐ SALTY

SAUCE

- ☐ SWEET
- ☐ TANGY
- ☐ THIN
- ☐ SAVORY
- ☐ SPICY
- ☐ CHUNKY

FRESHNESS ① ② ③ ④ ⑤   CRUST ① ② ③ ④ ⑤

CRUST

- ☐ BUTTERY
- ☐ CRISPY
- ☐ SPONGY
- ☐ BUBBLY
- ☐ CHEWY
- ☐ OTHER...........

NOTES

....
....
....

WOULD YOU TRY AGAIN?

☐ YES   ☐ NO

OVERALL RATING

★ ★ ★ ★ ★

Pizza Tasting Journal

DATE ▨▨▨▨▨   PIZZERIA ▨▨▨▨▨

NEIGHBOURHOOD ▨▨▨▨▨

BEVERAGE PAIRING ▨▨▨▨▨

TOPPINGS

- ☐ CHEESE
- ☐ MUSHROOMS
- ☐ GREEN PEPPER
- ☐ OTHER ....

- ☐ ONIONS
- ☐ BACON
- ☐ SAUSAGE

- ☐ PINEAPPLE
- ☐ TUNA
- ☐ BLACK OLIVES

CHEESE

- ☐ GREASY
- ☐ STINGY

- ☐ SMOKEY
- ☐ STINKY

- ☐ CREAMY
- ☐ SALTY

SAUCE

- ☐ SWEET
- ☐ TANGY

- ☐ THIN
- ☐ SAVORY

- ☐ SPICY
- ☐ CHUNKY

FRESHNESS ① ② ③ ④ ⑤   CRUST ① ② ③ ④ ⑤

CRUST

- ☐ BUTTERY
- ☐ CRISPY

- ☐ SPONGY
- ☐ BUBBLY

- ☐ CHEWY
- ☐ OTHER...........

NOTES

....
....
....

WOULD YOU TRY AGAIN?
☐ YES   ☐ NO

OVERALL RATING
★ ★ ★ ★ ★

Pizza Tasting Journal

DATE _____ PIZZERIA _____

NEIGHBOURHOOD _____

BEVERAGE PAIRING _____

TOPPINGS

- ☐ CHEESE
- ☐ MUSHROOMS
- ☐ GREEN PEPPER
- ☐ OTHER ....
- ☐ ONIONS
- ☐ BACON
- ☐ SAUSAGE
- ☐ PINEAPPLE
- ☐ TUNA
- ☐ BLACK OLIVES

CHEESE

- ☐ GREASY
- ☐ STINGY
- ☐ SMOKEY
- ☐ STINKY
- ☐ CREAMY
- ☐ SALTY

SAUCE

- ☐ SWEET
- ☐ TANGY
- ☐ THIN
- ☐ SAVORY
- ☐ SPICY
- ☐ CHUNKY

FRESHNESS ① ② ③ ④ ⑤   CRUST ① ② ③ ④ ⑤

CRUST

- ☐ BUTTERY
- ☐ CRISPY
- ☐ SPONGY
- ☐ BUBBLY
- ☐ CHEWY
- ☐ OTHER...........

NOTES

....
....
....

WOULD YOU TRY AGAIN?

☐ YES   ☐ NO

OVERALL RATING

★ ★ ★ ★ ★

Pizza Tasting Journal

DATE _____   PIZZERIA _____

NEIGHBOURHOOD _____

BEVERAGE PAIRING _____

TOPPINGS

☐ CHEESE   ☐ ONIONS   ☐ PINEAPPLE
☐ MUSHROOMS   ☐ BACON   ☐ TUNA
☐ GREEN PEPPER ☐ SAUSAGE   ☐ BLACK OLIVES
☐ OTHER ....

CHEESE

☐ GREASY   ☐ SMOKEY   ☐ CREAMY
☐ STINGY   ☐ STINKY   ☐ SALTY

SAUCE

☐ SWEET   ☐ THIN   ☐ SPICY
☐ TANGY   ☐ SAVORY   ☐ CHUNKY

FRESHNESS ① ② ③ ④ ⑤   CRUST ① ② ③ ④ ⑤

CRUST

☐ BUTTERY   ☐ SPONGY   ☐ CHEWY
☐ CRISPY   ☐ BUBBLY   ☐ OTHER..........

NOTES

....
....
....

WOULD YOU TRY AGAIN?
☐ YES   ☐ NO

OVERALL RATING
★ ★ ★ ★ ★

Pizza Tasting Journal

DATE _____ PIZZERIA _____

NEIGHBOURHOOD _____

BEVERAGE PAIRING _____

TOPPINGS

- [ ] CHEESE
- [ ] MUSHROOMS
- [ ] GREEN PEPPER
- [ ] OTHER ....

- [ ] ONIONS
- [ ] BACON
- [ ] SAUSAGE

- [ ] PINEAPPLE
- [ ] TUNA
- [ ] BLACK OLIVES

CHEESE

- [ ] GREASY
- [ ] STINGY

- [ ] SMOKEY
- [ ] STINKY

- [ ] CREAMY
- [ ] SALTY

SAUCE

- [ ] SWEET
- [ ] TANGY

- [ ] THIN
- [ ] SAVORY

- [ ] SPICY
- [ ] CHUNKY

FRESHNESS ① ② ③ ④ ⑤   CRUST ① ② ③ ④ ⑤

CRUST

- [ ] BUTTERY
- [ ] CRISPY

- [ ] SPONGY
- [ ] BUBBLY

- [ ] CHEWY
- [ ] OTHER...........

NOTES

....
....
....

WOULD YOU TRY AGAIN?
- [ ] YES
- [ ] NO

OVERALL RATING
☆ ☆ ☆ ☆ ☆

Pizza Tasting Journal

DATE [   ]   PIZZERIA [   ]

NEIGHBOURHOOD [   ]

BEVERAGE PAIRING [   ]

TOPPINGS

- ☐ CHEESE
- ☐ MUSHROOMS
- ☐ GREEN PEPPER
- ☐ OTHER ....

- ☐ ONIONS
- ☐ BACON
- ☐ SAUSAGE

- ☐ PINEAPPLE
- ☐ TUNA
- ☐ BLACK OLIVES

CHEESE

- ☐ GREASY
- ☐ STINGY

- ☐ SMOKEY
- ☐ STINKY

- ☐ CREAMY
- ☐ SALTY

SAUCE

- ☐ SWEET
- ☐ TANGY

- ☐ THIN
- ☐ SAVORY

- ☐ SPICY
- ☐ CHUNKY

FRESHNESS ① ② ③ ④ ⑤   CRUST ① ② ③ ④ ⑤

CRUST

- ☐ BUTTERY
- ☐ CRISPY

- ☐ SPONGY
- ☐ BUBBLY

- ☐ CHEWY
- ☐ OTHER...........

NOTES

....
....
....

WOULD YOU TRY AGAIN?
☐ YES   ☐ NO

OVERALL RATING
★ ★ ★ ★ ★

Pizza Tasting Journal

DATE _____ PIZZERIA _____

NEIGHBOURHOOD _____

BEVERAGE PAIRING _____

TOPPINGS

- ☐ CHEESE
- ☐ MUSHROOMS
- ☐ GREEN PEPPER
- ☐ OTHER ....
- ☐ ONIONS
- ☐ BACON
- ☐ SAUSAGE
- ☐ PINEAPPLE
- ☐ TUNA
- ☐ BLACK OLIVES

CHEESE

- ☐ GREASY
- ☐ STINGY
- ☐ SMOKEY
- ☐ STINKY
- ☐ CREAMY
- ☐ SALTY

SAUCE

- ☐ SWEET
- ☐ TANGY
- ☐ THIN
- ☐ SAVORY
- ☐ SPICY
- ☐ CHUNKY

FRESHNESS ① ② ③ ④ ⑤   CRUST ① ② ③ ④ ⑤

CRUST

- ☐ BUTTERY
- ☐ CRISPY
- ☐ SPONGY
- ☐ BUBBLY
- ☐ CHEWY
- ☐ OTHER...........

NOTES

....
....
....

WOULD YOU TRY AGAIN?
☐ YES   ☐ NO

OVERALL RATING
☆ ☆ ☆ ☆ ☆

Pizza Tasting Journal

DATE _____ PIZZERIA _____

NEIGHBOURHOOD _____

BEVERAGE PAIRING _____

TOPPINGS

- ☐ CHEESE
- ☐ MUSHROOMS
- ☐ GREEN PEPPER
- ☐ OTHER ....
- ☐ ONIONS
- ☐ BACON
- ☐ SAUSAGE
- ☐ PINEAPPLE
- ☐ TUNA
- ☐ BLACK OLIVES

CHEESE

- ☐ GREASY
- ☐ STINGY
- ☐ SMOKEY
- ☐ STINKY
- ☐ CREAMY
- ☐ SALTY

SAUCE

- ☐ SWEET
- ☐ TANGY
- ☐ THIN
- ☐ SAVORY
- ☐ SPICY
- ☐ CHUNKY

FRESHNESS ① ② ③ ④ ⑤   CRUST ① ② ③ ④ ⑤

CRUST

- ☐ BUTTERY
- ☐ CRISPY
- ☐ SPONGY
- ☐ BUBBLY
- ☐ CHEWY
- ☐ OTHER...........

NOTES

....
....
....

WOULD YOU TRY AGAIN?
- ☐ YES
- ☐ NO

OVERALL RATING
★ ★ ★ ★ ★

Pizza Tasting Journal

DATE _____   PIZZERIA _____

NEIGHBOURHOOD _____

BEVERAGE PAIRING _____

TOPPINGS

- ☐ CHEESE
- ☐ MUSHROOMS
- ☐ GREEN PEPPER
- ☐ OTHER ....

- ☐ ONIONS
- ☐ BACON
- ☐ SAUSAGE

- ☐ PINEAPPLE
- ☐ TUNA
- ☐ BLACK OLIVES

CHEESE

- ☐ GREASY
- ☐ STINGY

- ☐ SMOKEY
- ☐ STINKY

- ☐ CREAMY
- ☐ SALTY

SAUCE

- ☐ SWEET
- ☐ TANGY

- ☐ THIN
- ☐ SAVORY

- ☐ SPICY
- ☐ CHUNKY

FRESHNESS ① ② ③ ④ ⑤   CRUST ① ② ③ ④ ⑤

CRUST

- ☐ BUTTERY
- ☐ CRISPY

- ☐ SPONGY
- ☐ BUBBLY

- ☐ CHEWY
- ☐ OTHER............

NOTES

....
....
....

WOULD YOU TRY AGAIN?

☐ YES   ☐ NO

OVERALL RATING

★ ★ ★ ★ ★

Pizza Tasting Journal

DATE _____   PIZZERIA _____

NEIGHBOURHOOD _____

BEVERAGE PAIRING _____

TOPPINGS

- ☐ CHEESE
- ☐ MUSHROOMS
- ☐ GREEN PEPPER
- ☐ OTHER ....

- ☐ ONIONS
- ☐ BACON
- ☐ SAUSAGE

- ☐ PINEAPPLE
- ☐ TUNA
- ☐ BLACK OLIVES

CHEESE

- ☐ GREASY
- ☐ STINGY

- ☐ SMOKEY
- ☐ STINKY

- ☐ CREAMY
- ☐ SALTY

SAUCE

- ☐ SWEET
- ☐ TANGY

- ☐ THIN
- ☐ SAVORY

- ☐ SPICY
- ☐ CHUNKY

FRESHNESS ① ② ③ ④ ⑤   CRUST ① ② ③ ④ ⑤

CRUST

- ☐ BUTTERY
- ☐ CRISPY

- ☐ SPONGY
- ☐ BUBBLY

- ☐ CHEWY
- ☐ OTHER............

NOTES

....
....
....

WOULD YOU TRY AGAIN?
☐ YES   ☐ NO

OVERALL RATING
★ ★ ★ ★ ★

Pizza Tasting Journal

DATE _____ PIZZERIA _____

NEIGHBOURHOOD _____

BEVERAGE PAIRING _____

TOPPINGS

- [ ] CHEESE
- [ ] MUSHROOMS
- [ ] GREEN PEPPER
- [ ] OTHER ....

- [ ] ONIONS
- [ ] BACON
- [ ] SAUSAGE

- [ ] PINEAPPLE
- [ ] TUNA
- [ ] BLACK OLIVES

CHEESE

- [ ] GREASY
- [ ] STINGY

- [ ] SMOKEY
- [ ] STINKY

- [ ] CREAMY
- [ ] SALTY

SAUCE

- [ ] SWEET
- [ ] TANGY

- [ ] THIN
- [ ] SAVORY

- [ ] SPICY
- [ ] CHUNKY

FRESHNESS ① ② ③ ④ ⑤   CRUST ① ② ③ ④ ⑤

CRUST

- [ ] BUTTERY
- [ ] CRISPY

- [ ] SPONGY
- [ ] BUBBLY

- [ ] CHEWY
- [ ] OTHER...........

NOTES

....
....
....

WOULD YOU TRY AGAIN?
- [ ] YES   - [ ] NO

OVERALL RATING
☆ ☆ ☆ ☆ ☆

Pizza Tasting Journal

DATE _____ PIZZERIA _____

NEIGHBOURHOOD _____

BEVERAGE PAIRING _____

TOPPINGS

☐ CHEESE   ☐ ONIONS   ☐ PINEAPPLE
☐ MUSHROOMS   ☐ BACON   ☐ TUNA
☐ GREEN PEPPER   ☐ SAUSAGE   ☐ BLACK OLIVES
☐ OTHER ....

CHEESE

☐ GREASY   ☐ SMOKEY   ☐ CREAMY
☐ STINGY   ☐ STINKY   ☐ SALTY

SAUCE

☐ SWEET   ☐ THIN   ☐ SPICY
☐ TANGY   ☐ SAVORY   ☐ CHUNKY

FRESHNESS ① ② ③ ④ ⑤   CRUST ① ② ③ ④ ⑤

CRUST

☐ BUTTERY   ☐ SPONGY   ☐ CHEWY
☐ CRISPY   ☐ BUBBLY   ☐ OTHER...........

NOTES

....
....
....

WOULD YOU TRY AGAIN?   **OVERALL RATING**
☐ YES   ☐ NO   ★ ★ ★ ★ ★

Pizza Tasting Journal

DATE _____ PIZZERIA _____

NEIGHBOURHOOD _____

BEVERAGE PAIRING _____

TOPPINGS

- [ ] CHEESE
- [ ] MUSHROOMS
- [ ] GREEN PEPPER
- [ ] OTHER ....

- [ ] ONIONS
- [ ] BACON
- [ ] SAUSAGE

- [ ] PINEAPPLE
- [ ] TUNA
- [ ] BLACK OLIVES

CHEESE

- [ ] GREASY
- [ ] STINGY

- [ ] SMOKEY
- [ ] STINKY

- [ ] CREAMY
- [ ] SALTY

SAUCE

- [ ] SWEET
- [ ] TANGY

- [ ] THIN
- [ ] SAVORY

- [ ] SPICY
- [ ] CHUNKY

FRESHNESS (1) (2) (3) (4) (5)   CRUST (1) (2) (3) (4) (5)

CRUST

- [ ] BUTTERY
- [ ] CRISPY

- [ ] SPONGY
- [ ] BUBBLY

- [ ] CHEWY
- [ ] OTHER............

NOTES

....
....
....

WOULD YOU TRY AGAIN?

- [ ] YES
- [ ] NO

OVERALL RATING

⭐ ⭐ ⭐ ⭐ ⭐

Pizza Tasting Journal

DATE _____ PIZZERIA _____

NEIGHBOURHOOD _____

BEVERAGE PAIRING _____

TOPPINGS

- ☐ CHEESE
- ☐ MUSHROOMS
- ☐ GREEN PEPPER
- ☐ OTHER ....

- ☐ ONIONS
- ☐ BACON
- ☐ SAUSAGE

- ☐ PINEAPPLE
- ☐ TUNA
- ☐ BLACK OLIVES

CHEESE

- ☐ GREASY
- ☐ STINGY

- ☐ SMOKEY
- ☐ STINKY

- ☐ CREAMY
- ☐ SALTY

SAUCE

- ☐ SWEET
- ☐ TANGY

- ☐ THIN
- ☐ SAVORY

- ☐ SPICY
- ☐ CHUNKY

FRESHNESS ① ② ③ ④ ⑤   CRUST ① ② ③ ④ ⑤

CRUST

- ☐ BUTTERY
- ☐ CRISPY

- ☐ SPONGY
- ☐ BUBBLY

- ☐ CHEWY
- ☐ OTHER...........

NOTES

....
....
....

WOULD YOU TRY AGAIN?
☐ YES   ☐ NO

OVERALL RATING
★ ★ ★ ★ ★

Pizza Tasting Journal

DATE _____   PIZZERIA _____

NEIGHBOURHOOD _____

BEVERAGE PAIRING _____

TOPPINGS

- [ ] CHEESE
- [ ] MUSHROOMS
- [ ] GREEN PEPPER
- [ ] OTHER ....

- [ ] ONIONS
- [ ] BACON
- [ ] SAUSAGE

- [ ] PINEAPPLE
- [ ] TUNA
- [ ] BLACK OLIVES

CHEESE

- [ ] GREASY
- [ ] STINGY

- [ ] SMOKEY
- [ ] STINKY

- [ ] CREAMY
- [ ] SALTY

SAUCE

- [ ] SWEET
- [ ] TANGY

- [ ] THIN
- [ ] SAVORY

- [ ] SPICY
- [ ] CHUNKY

FRESHNESS (1) (2) (3) (4) (5)   CRUST (1) (2) (3) (4) (5)

CRUST

- [ ] BUTTERY
- [ ] CRISPY

- [ ] SPONGY
- [ ] BUBBLY

- [ ] CHEWY
- [ ] OTHER...........

NOTES

....
....
....

WOULD YOU TRY AGAIN?

- [ ] YES   - [ ] NO

OVERALL RATING

☆ ☆ ☆ ☆ ☆

Pizza Tasting Journal

DATE _____ PIZZERIA _____

NEIGHBOURHOOD _____

BEVERAGE PAIRING _____

TOPPINGS

☐ CHEESE ☐ ONIONS ☐ PINEAPPLE
☐ MUSHROOMS ☐ BACON ☐ TUNA
☐ GREEN PEPPER ☐ SAUSAGE ☐ BLACK OLIVES
☐ OTHER ....

CHEESE

☐ GREASY ☐ SMOKEY ☐ CREAMY
☐ STINGY ☐ STINKY ☐ SALTY

SAUCE

☐ SWEET ☐ THIN ☐ SPICY
☐ TANGY ☐ SAVORY ☐ CHUNKY

FRESHNESS ① ② ③ ④ ⑤   CRUST ① ② ③ ④ ⑤

CRUST

☐ BUTTERY ☐ SPONGY ☐ CHEWY
☐ CRISPY ☐ BUBBLY ☐ OTHER...........

NOTES

....
....
....

WOULD YOU TRY AGAIN?   **OVERALL RATING**

☐ YES   ☐ NO   ☆ ☆ ☆ ☆ ☆

Pizza Tasting Journal

DATE _____   PIZZERIA _____

NEIGHBOURHOOD _____

BEVERAGE PAIRING _____

TOPPINGS

- ☐ CHEESE
- ☐ MUSHROOMS
- ☐ GREEN PEPPER
- ☐ OTHER ....

- ☐ ONIONS
- ☐ BACON
- ☐ SAUSAGE

- ☐ PINEAPPLE
- ☐ TUNA
- ☐ BLACK OLIVES

CHEESE

- ☐ GREASY
- ☐ STINGY

- ☐ SMOKEY
- ☐ STINKY

- ☐ CREAMY
- ☐ SALTY

SAUCE

- ☐ SWEET
- ☐ TANGY

- ☐ THIN
- ☐ SAVORY

- ☐ SPICY
- ☐ CHUNKY

FRESHNESS ① ② ③ ④ ⑤   CRUST ① ② ③ ④ ⑤

CRUST

- ☐ BUTTERY
- ☐ CRISPY

- ☐ SPONGY
- ☐ BUBBLY

- ☐ CHEWY
- ☐ OTHER............

NOTES

....
....
....

WOULD YOU TRY AGAIN?

☐ YES   ☐ NO

OVERALL RATING

★ ★ ★ ★ ★

Pizza Tasting Journal

DATE _____   PIZZERIA _____

NEIGHBOURHOOD _____

BEVERAGE PAIRING _____

TOPPINGS

- ☐ CHEESE
- ☐ MUSHROOMS
- ☐ GREEN PEPPER
- ☐ OTHER ....

- ☐ ONIONS
- ☐ BACON
- ☐ SAUSAGE

- ☐ PINEAPPLE
- ☐ TUNA
- ☐ BLACK OLIVES

CHEESE

- ☐ GREASY
- ☐ STINGY

- ☐ SMOKEY
- ☐ STINKY

- ☐ CREAMY
- ☐ SALTY

SAUCE

- ☐ SWEET
- ☐ TANGY

- ☐ THIN
- ☐ SAVORY

- ☐ SPICY
- ☐ CHUNKY

FRESHNESS ① ② ③ ④ ⑤   CRUST ① ② ③ ④ ⑤

CRUST

- ☐ BUTTERY
- ☐ CRISPY

- ☐ SPONGY
- ☐ BUBBLY

- ☐ CHEWY
- ☐ OTHER...........

NOTES

....
....
....

WOULD YOU TRY AGAIN?
- ☐ YES   ☐ NO

OVERALL RATING
★ ★ ★ ★ ★

Pizza Tasting Journal

DATE _____   PIZZERIA _____

NEIGHBOURHOOD _____

BEVERAGE PAIRING _____

TOPPINGS

- [ ] CHEESE
- [ ] MUSHROOMS
- [ ] GREEN PEPPER
- [ ] OTHER ....

- [ ] ONIONS
- [ ] BACON
- [ ] SAUSAGE

- [ ] PINEAPPLE
- [ ] TUNA
- [ ] BLACK OLIVES

CHEESE

- [ ] GREASY
- [ ] STINGY

- [ ] SMOKEY
- [ ] STINKY

- [ ] CREAMY
- [ ] SALTY

SAUCE

- [ ] SWEET
- [ ] TANGY

- [ ] THIN
- [ ] SAVORY

- [ ] SPICY
- [ ] CHUNKY

FRESHNESS ① ② ③ ④ ⑤   CRUST ① ② ③ ④ ⑤

CRUST

- [ ] BUTTERY
- [ ] CRISPY

- [ ] SPONGY
- [ ] BUBBLY

- [ ] CHEWY
- [ ] OTHER............

NOTES

....
....
....

WOULD YOU TRY AGAIN?
- [ ] YES   - [ ] NO

OVERALL RATING
★ ★ ★ ★ ★

Pizza Tasting Journal

DATE ⬚⬚⬚⬚⬚ PIZZERIA ⬚⬚⬚⬚⬚

NEIGHBOURHOOD ⬚⬚⬚⬚⬚

BEVERAGE PAIRING ⬚⬚⬚⬚⬚

TOPPINGS

- ☐ CHEESE
- ☐ MUSHROOMS
- ☐ GREEN PEPPER
- ☐ OTHER ....
- ☐ ONIONS
- ☐ BACON
- ☐ SAUSAGE
- ☐ PINEAPPLE
- ☐ TUNA
- ☐ BLACK OLIVES

CHEESE

- ☐ GREASY
- ☐ STINGY
- ☐ SMOKEY
- ☐ STINKY
- ☐ CREAMY
- ☐ SALTY

SAUCE

- ☐ SWEET
- ☐ TANGY
- ☐ THIN
- ☐ SAVORY
- ☐ SPICY
- ☐ CHUNKY

FRESHNESS ① ② ③ ④ ⑤   CRUST ① ② ③ ④ ⑤

CRUST

- ☐ BUTTERY
- ☐ CRISPY
- ☐ SPONGY
- ☐ BUBBLY
- ☐ CHEWY
- ☐ OTHER...........

NOTES

....
....
....

WOULD YOU TRY AGAIN?
☐ YES   ☐ NO

OVERALL RATING
★ ★ ★ ★ ★

Pizza Tasting Journal

DATE _____ PIZZERIA _____

NEIGHBOURHOOD _____

BEVERAGE PAIRING _____

TOPPINGS

- ☐ CHEESE
- ☐ MUSHROOMS
- ☐ GREEN PEPPER
- ☐ OTHER ....

- ☐ ONIONS
- ☐ BACON
- ☐ SAUSAGE

- ☐ PINEAPPLE
- ☐ TUNA
- ☐ BLACK OLIVES

CHEESE

- ☐ GREASY
- ☐ STINGY

- ☐ SMOKEY
- ☐ STINKY

- ☐ CREAMY
- ☐ SALTY

SAUCE

- ☐ SWEET
- ☐ TANGY

- ☐ THIN
- ☐ SAVORY

- ☐ SPICY
- ☐ CHUNKY

FRESHNESS ① ② ③ ④ ⑤   CRUST ① ② ③ ④ ⑤

CRUST

- ☐ BUTTERY
- ☐ CRISPY

- ☐ SPONGY
- ☐ BUBBLY

- ☐ CHEWY
- ☐ OTHER...........

NOTES

....
....
....

WOULD YOU TRY AGAIN?

☐ YES   ☐ NO

OVERALL RATING

☆ ☆ ☆ ☆ ☆

Pizza Tasting Journal

DATE ▭   PIZZERIA ▭

NEIGHBOURHOOD ▭

BEVERAGE PAIRING ▭

TOPPINGS

☐ CHEESE   ☐ ONIONS   ☐ PINEAPPLE
☐ MUSHROOMS   ☐ BACON   ☐ TUNA
☐ GREEN PEPPER ☐ SAUSAGE   ☐ BLACK OLIVES
☐ OTHER ....

CHEESE

☐ GREASY   ☐ SMOKEY   ☐ CREAMY
☐ STINGY   ☐ STINKY   ☐ SALTY

SAUCE

☐ SWEET   ☐ THIN   ☐ SPICY
☐ TANGY   ☐ SAVORY   ☐ CHUNKY

FRESHNESS ① ② ③ ④ ⑤   CRUST ① ② ③ ④ ⑤

CRUST

☐ BUTTERY   ☐ SPONGY   ☐ CHEWY
☐ CRISPY   ☐ BUBBLY   ☐ OTHER...........

NOTES

....
....
....

WOULD YOU TRY AGAIN?   **OVERALL RATING**
☐ YES   ☐ NO   ★ ★ ★ ★ ★

Pizza Tasting Journal

DATE _____ PIZZERIA _____

NEIGHBOURHOOD _____

BEVERAGE PAIRING _____

TOPPINGS

- ☐ CHEESE
- ☐ MUSHROOMS
- ☐ GREEN PEPPER
- ☐ OTHER ....
- ☐ ONIONS
- ☐ BACON
- ☐ SAUSAGE
- ☐ PINEAPPLE
- ☐ TUNA
- ☐ BLACK OLIVES

CHEESE

- ☐ GREASY
- ☐ STINGY
- ☐ SMOKEY
- ☐ STINKY
- ☐ CREAMY
- ☐ SALTY

SAUCE

- ☐ SWEET
- ☐ TANGY
- ☐ THIN
- ☐ SAVORY
- ☐ SPICY
- ☐ CHUNKY

FRESHNESS ① ② ③ ④ ⑤   CRUST ① ② ③ ④ ⑤

CRUST

- ☐ BUTTERY
- ☐ CRISPY
- ☐ SPONGY
- ☐ BUBBLY
- ☐ CHEWY
- ☐ OTHER............

NOTES

....
....
....

WOULD YOU TRY AGAIN?

☐ YES   ☐ NO

OVERALL RATING

★ ★ ★ ★ ★

Pizza Tasting Journal

DATE _____   PIZZERIA _____

NEIGHBOURHOOD _____

BEVERAGE PAIRING _____

TOPPINGS

- ☐ CHEESE
- ☐ MUSHROOMS
- ☐ GREEN PEPPER
- ☐ OTHER ....
- ☐ ONIONS
- ☐ BACON
- ☐ SAUSAGE
- ☐ PINEAPPLE
- ☐ TUNA
- ☐ BLACK OLIVES

CHEESE

- ☐ GREASY
- ☐ STINGY
- ☐ SMOKEY
- ☐ STINKY
- ☐ CREAMY
- ☐ SALTY

SAUCE

- ☐ SWEET
- ☐ TANGY
- ☐ THIN
- ☐ SAVORY
- ☐ SPICY
- ☐ CHUNKY

FRESHNESS ① ② ③ ④ ⑤   CRUST ① ② ③ ④ ⑤

CRUST

- ☐ BUTTERY
- ☐ CRISPY
- ☐ SPONGY
- ☐ BUBBLY
- ☐ CHEWY
- ☐ OTHER...........

NOTES

....
....
....

WOULD YOU TRY AGAIN?
☐ YES   ☐ NO

OVERALL RATING
★ ★ ★ ★ ★

Pizza Tasting Journal

DATE _____ PIZZERIA _____

NEIGHBOURHOOD _____

BEVERAGE PAIRING _____

TOPPINGS

☐ CHEESE   ☐ ONIONS   ☐ PINEAPPLE
☐ MUSHROOMS   ☐ BACON   ☐ TUNA
☐ GREEN PEPPER   ☐ SAUSAGE   ☐ BLACK OLIVES
☐ OTHER ....

CHEESE

☐ GREASY   ☐ SMOKEY   ☐ CREAMY
☐ STINGY   ☐ STINKY   ☐ SALTY

SAUCE

☐ SWEET   ☐ THIN   ☐ SPICY
☐ TANGY   ☐ SAVORY   ☐ CHUNKY

FRESHNESS ① ② ③ ④ ⑤   CRUST ① ② ③ ④ ⑤

CRUST

☐ BUTTERY   ☐ SPONGY   ☐ CHEWY
☐ CRISPY   ☐ BUBBLY   ☐ OTHER...........

NOTES

....
....
....

WOULD YOU TRY AGAIN?   **OVERALL RATING**
☐ YES   ☐ NO   ☆ ☆ ☆ ☆ ☆

Pizza Tasting Journal

DATE _____ PIZZERIA _____

NEIGHBOURHOOD _____

BEVERAGE PAIRING _____

TOPPINGS

- ☐ CHEESE
- ☐ MUSHROOMS
- ☐ GREEN PEPPER
- ☐ OTHER ....
- ☐ ONIONS
- ☐ BACON
- ☐ SAUSAGE
- ☐ PINEAPPLE
- ☐ TUNA
- ☐ BLACK OLIVES

CHEESE

- ☐ GREASY
- ☐ STINGY
- ☐ SMOKEY
- ☐ STINKY
- ☐ CREAMY
- ☐ SALTY

SAUCE

- ☐ SWEET
- ☐ TANGY
- ☐ THIN
- ☐ SAVORY
- ☐ SPICY
- ☐ CHUNKY

FRESHNESS ① ② ③ ④ ⑤   CRUST ① ② ③ ④ ⑤

CRUST

- ☐ BUTTERY
- ☐ CRISPY
- ☐ SPONGY
- ☐ BUBBLY
- ☐ CHEWY
- ☐ OTHER...........

NOTES

....
....
....

WOULD YOU TRY AGAIN?

☐ YES   ☐ NO

OVERALL RATING

★ ★ ★ ★ ★

Pizza Tasting Journal

DATE _____ PIZZERIA _____

NEIGHBOURHOOD _____

BEVERAGE PAIRING _____

TOPPINGS

- ☐ CHEESE
- ☐ MUSHROOMS
- ☐ GREEN PEPPER
- ☐ OTHER ....
- ☐ ONIONS
- ☐ BACON
- ☐ SAUSAGE
- ☐ PINEAPPLE
- ☐ TUNA
- ☐ BLACK OLIVES

CHEESE

- ☐ GREASY
- ☐ STINGY
- ☐ SMOKEY
- ☐ STINKY
- ☐ CREAMY
- ☐ SALTY

SAUCE

- ☐ SWEET
- ☐ TANGY
- ☐ THIN
- ☐ SAVORY
- ☐ SPICY
- ☐ CHUNKY

FRESHNESS ① ② ③ ④ ⑤   CRUST ① ② ③ ④ ⑤

CRUST

- ☐ BUTTERY
- ☐ CRISPY
- ☐ SPONGY
- ☐ BUBBLY
- ☐ CHEWY
- ☐ OTHER............

NOTES

....
....
....

WOULD YOU TRY AGAIN?   **OVERALL RATING**

☐ YES   ☐ NO   ☆ ☆ ☆ ☆ ☆

Pizza Tasting Journal

DATE _____   PIZZERIA _____

NEIGHBOURHOOD _____

BEVERAGE PAIRING _____

TOPPINGS

- ☐ CHEESE
- ☐ MUSHROOMS
- ☐ GREEN PEPPER
- ☐ OTHER ....
- ☐ ONIONS
- ☐ BACON
- ☐ SAUSAGE
- ☐ PINEAPPLE
- ☐ TUNA
- ☐ BLACK OLIVES

CHEESE

- ☐ GREASY
- ☐ STINGY
- ☐ SMOKEY
- ☐ STINKY
- ☐ CREAMY
- ☐ SALTY

SAUCE

- ☐ SWEET
- ☐ TANGY
- ☐ THIN
- ☐ SAVORY
- ☐ SPICY
- ☐ CHUNKY

FRESHNESS ① ② ③ ④ ⑤   CRUST ① ② ③ ④ ⑤

CRUST

- ☐ BUTTERY
- ☐ CRISPY
- ☐ SPONGY
- ☐ BUBBLY
- ☐ CHEWY
- ☐ OTHER............

NOTES

....
....
....

WOULD YOU TRY AGAIN?
☐ YES   ☐ NO

OVERALL RATING
★ ★ ★ ★ ★

Pizza Tasting Journal

DATE _____ PIZZERIA _____

NEIGHBOURHOOD _____

BEVERAGE PAIRING _____

TOPPINGS

☐ CHEESE   ☐ ONIONS   ☐ PINEAPPLE
☐ MUSHROOMS   ☐ BACON   ☐ TUNA
☐ GREEN PEPPER   ☐ SAUSAGE   ☐ BLACK OLIVES
☐ OTHER ....

CHEESE

☐ GREASY   ☐ SMOKEY   ☐ CREAMY
☐ STINGY   ☐ STINKY   ☐ SALTY

SAUCE

☐ SWEET   ☐ THIN   ☐ SPICY
☐ TANGY   ☐ SAVORY   ☐ CHUNKY

FRESHNESS ① ② ③ ④ ⑤   CRUST ① ② ③ ④ ⑤

CRUST

☐ BUTTERY   ☐ SPONGY   ☐ CHEWY
☐ CRISPY   ☐ BUBBLY   ☐ OTHER...........

NOTES

....
....
....

WOULD YOU TRY AGAIN?   **OVERALL RATING**

☐ YES   ☐ NO   ★ ★ ★ ★ ★

Pizza Tasting Journal

DATE _____ PIZZERIA _____

NEIGHBOURHOOD _____

BEVERAGE PAIRING _____

TOPPINGS

- ☐ CHEESE
- ☐ MUSHROOMS
- ☐ GREEN PEPPER
- ☐ OTHER ....

- ☐ ONIONS
- ☐ BACON
- ☐ SAUSAGE

- ☐ PINEAPPLE
- ☐ TUNA
- ☐ BLACK OLIVES

CHEESE

- ☐ GREASY
- ☐ STINGY

- ☐ SMOKEY
- ☐ STINKY

- ☐ CREAMY
- ☐ SALTY

SAUCE

- ☐ SWEET
- ☐ TANGY

- ☐ THIN
- ☐ SAVORY

- ☐ SPICY
- ☐ CHUNKY

FRESHNESS ① ② ③ ④ ⑤   CRUST ① ② ③ ④ ⑤

CRUST

- ☐ BUTTERY
- ☐ CRISPY

- ☐ SPONGY
- ☐ BUBBLY

- ☐ CHEWY
- ☐ OTHER...........

NOTES

....
....
....

WOULD YOU TRY AGAIN?
☐ YES   ☐ NO

OVERALL RATING
★ ★ ★ ★ ★

Pizza Tasting Journal

DATE _____ PIZZERIA _____

NEIGHBOURHOOD _____

BEVERAGE PAIRING _____

TOPPINGS

- ☐ CHEESE
- ☐ MUSHROOMS
- ☐ GREEN PEPPER
- ☐ OTHER ....

- ☐ ONIONS
- ☐ BACON
- ☐ SAUSAGE

- ☐ PINEAPPLE
- ☐ TUNA
- ☐ BLACK OLIVES

CHEESE

- ☐ GREASY
- ☐ STINGY

- ☐ SMOKEY
- ☐ STINKY

- ☐ CREAMY
- ☐ SALTY

SAUCE

- ☐ SWEET
- ☐ TANGY

- ☐ THIN
- ☐ SAVORY

- ☐ SPICY
- ☐ CHUNKY

FRESHNESS ① ② ③ ④ ⑤   CRUST ① ② ③ ④ ⑤

CRUST

- ☐ BUTTERY
- ☐ CRISPY

- ☐ SPONGY
- ☐ BUBBLY

- ☐ CHEWY
- ☐ OTHER............

NOTES

....
....
....

WOULD YOU TRY AGAIN?

☐ YES   ☐ NO

OVERALL RATING

☆ ☆ ☆ ☆ ☆

Pizza Tasting Journal

DATE _____ PIZZERIA _____

NEIGHBOURHOOD _____

BEVERAGE PAIRING _____

TOPPINGS

- [ ] CHEESE
- [ ] MUSHROOMS
- [ ] GREEN PEPPER
- [ ] OTHER ....
- [ ] ONIONS
- [ ] BACON
- [ ] SAUSAGE
- [ ] PINEAPPLE
- [ ] TUNA
- [ ] BLACK OLIVES

CHEESE

- [ ] GREASY
- [ ] STINGY
- [ ] SMOKEY
- [ ] STINKY
- [ ] CREAMY
- [ ] SALTY

SAUCE

- [ ] SWEET
- [ ] TANGY
- [ ] THIN
- [ ] SAVORY
- [ ] SPICY
- [ ] CHUNKY

FRESHNESS ① ② ③ ④ ⑤   CRUST ① ② ③ ④ ⑤

CRUST

- [ ] BUTTERY
- [ ] CRISPY
- [ ] SPONGY
- [ ] BUBBLY
- [ ] CHEWY
- [ ] OTHER...........

NOTES

....
....
....

WOULD YOU TRY AGAIN?

- [ ] YES
- [ ] NO

OVERALL RATING

⭐ ⭐ ⭐ ⭐ ⭐

Pizza Tasting Journal

DATE _____ PIZZERIA _____

NEIGHBOURHOOD _____

BEVERAGE PAIRING _____

TOPPINGS

☐ CHEESE ☐ ONIONS ☐ PINEAPPLE
☐ MUSHROOMS ☐ BACON ☐ TUNA
☐ GREEN PEPPER ☐ SAUSAGE ☐ BLACK OLIVES
☐ OTHER ....

CHEESE

☐ GREASY ☐ SMOKEY ☐ CREAMY
☐ STINGY ☐ STINKY ☐ SALTY

SAUCE

☐ SWEET ☐ THIN ☐ SPICY
☐ TANGY ☐ SAVORY ☐ CHUNKY

FRESHNESS ① ② ③ ④ ⑤   CRUST ① ② ③ ④ ⑤

CRUST

☐ BUTTERY ☐ SPONGY ☐ CHEWY
☐ CRISPY ☐ BUBBLY ☐ OTHER...........

NOTES

....
....
....

WOULD YOU TRY AGAIN?   **OVERALL RATING**

☐ YES   ☐ NO   ★ ★ ★ ★ ★

Pizza Tasting Journal

DATE [   ] PIZZERIA [   ]

NEIGHBOURHOOD [   ]

BEVERAGE PAIRING [   ]

TOPPINGS

- [ ] CHEESE
- [ ] MUSHROOMS
- [ ] GREEN PEPPER
- [ ] OTHER ....

- [ ] ONIONS
- [ ] BACON
- [ ] SAUSAGE

- [ ] PINEAPPLE
- [ ] TUNA
- [ ] BLACK OLIVES

CHEESE

- [ ] GREASY
- [ ] STINGY

- [ ] SMOKEY
- [ ] STINKY

- [ ] CREAMY
- [ ] SALTY

SAUCE

- [ ] SWEET
- [ ] TANGY

- [ ] THIN
- [ ] SAVORY

- [ ] SPICY
- [ ] CHUNKY

FRESHNESS ① ② ③ ④ ⑤   CRUST ① ② ③ ④ ⑤

CRUST

- [ ] BUTTERY
- [ ] CRISPY

- [ ] SPONGY
- [ ] BUBBLY

- [ ] CHEWY
- [ ] OTHER...........

NOTES

....
....
....

WOULD YOU TRY AGAIN?
- [ ] YES
- [ ] NO

OVERALL RATING
⭐ ⭐ ⭐ ⭐ ⭐

Pizza Tasting Journal

DATE _____ PIZZERIA _____

NEIGHBOURHOOD _____

BEVERAGE PAIRING _____

TOPPINGS

- [ ] CHEESE
- [ ] MUSHROOMS
- [ ] GREEN PEPPER
- [ ] OTHER ....

- [ ] ONIONS
- [ ] BACON
- [ ] SAUSAGE

- [ ] PINEAPPLE
- [ ] TUNA
- [ ] BLACK OLIVES

CHEESE

- [ ] GREASY
- [ ] STINGY

- [ ] SMOKEY
- [ ] STINKY

- [ ] CREAMY
- [ ] SALTY

SAUCE

- [ ] SWEET
- [ ] TANGY

- [ ] THIN
- [ ] SAVORY

- [ ] SPICY
- [ ] CHUNKY

FRESHNESS ① ② ③ ④ ⑤   CRUST ① ② ③ ④ ⑤

CRUST

- [ ] BUTTERY
- [ ] CRISPY

- [ ] SPONGY
- [ ] BUBBLY

- [ ] CHEWY
- [ ] OTHER...........

NOTES

....
....
....

WOULD YOU TRY AGAIN?

- [ ] YES   - [ ] NO

OVERALL RATING

★ ★ ★ ★ ★

Pizza Tasting Journal

DATE [   ] PIZZERIA [   ]

NEIGHBOURHOOD [   ]

BEVERAGE PAIRING [   ]

TOPPINGS

☐ CHEESE   ☐ ONIONS   ☐ PINEAPPLE
☐ MUSHROOMS   ☐ BACON   ☐ TUNA
☐ GREEN PEPPER   ☐ SAUSAGE   ☐ BLACK OLIVES
☐ OTHER ....

CHEESE

☐ GREASY   ☐ SMOKEY   ☐ CREAMY
☐ STINGY   ☐ STINKY   ☐ SALTY

SAUCE

☐ SWEET   ☐ THIN   ☐ SPICY
☐ TANGY   ☐ SAVORY   ☐ CHUNKY

FRESHNESS ① ② ③ ④ ⑤   CRUST ① ② ③ ④ ⑤

CRUST

☐ BUTTERY   ☐ SPONGY   ☐ CHEWY
☐ CRISPY   ☐ BUBBLY   ☐ OTHER............

NOTES

....
....
....

WOULD YOU TRY AGAIN?
☐ YES   ☐ NO

OVERALL RATING
★ ★ ★ ★ ★

Pizza Tasting Journal

DATE _____ PIZZERIA _____

NEIGHBOURHOOD _____

BEVERAGE PAIRING _____

TOPPINGS

- [ ] CHEESE
- [ ] MUSHROOMS
- [ ] GREEN PEPPER
- [ ] OTHER ....
- [ ] ONIONS
- [ ] BACON
- [ ] SAUSAGE
- [ ] PINEAPPLE
- [ ] TUNA
- [ ] BLACK OLIVES

CHEESE

- [ ] GREASY
- [ ] STINGY
- [ ] SMOKEY
- [ ] STINKY
- [ ] CREAMY
- [ ] SALTY

SAUCE

- [ ] SWEET
- [ ] TANGY
- [ ] THIN
- [ ] SAVORY
- [ ] SPICY
- [ ] CHUNKY

FRESHNESS ① ② ③ ④ ⑤   CRUST ① ② ③ ④ ⑤

CRUST

- [ ] BUTTERY
- [ ] CRISPY
- [ ] SPONGY
- [ ] BUBBLY
- [ ] CHEWY
- [ ] OTHER...........

NOTES

....
....
....

WOULD YOU TRY AGAIN?

- [ ] YES   - [ ] NO

OVERALL RATING

★ ★ ★ ★ ★

Pizza Tasting Journal

DATE _____ PIZZERIA _____

NEIGHBOURHOOD _____

BEVERAGE PAIRING _____

TOPPINGS

- ☐ CHEESE
- ☐ MUSHROOMS
- ☐ GREEN PEPPER
- ☐ OTHER ....

- ☐ ONIONS
- ☐ BACON
- ☐ SAUSAGE

- ☐ PINEAPPLE
- ☐ TUNA
- ☐ BLACK OLIVES

CHEESE

- ☐ GREASY
- ☐ STINGY

- ☐ SMOKEY
- ☐ STINKY

- ☐ CREAMY
- ☐ SALTY

SAUCE

- ☐ SWEET
- ☐ TANGY

- ☐ THIN
- ☐ SAVORY

- ☐ SPICY
- ☐ CHUNKY

FRESHNESS ① ② ③ ④ ⑤   CRUST ① ② ③ ④ ⑤

CRUST

- ☐ BUTTERY
- ☐ CRISPY

- ☐ SPONGY
- ☐ BUBBLY

- ☐ CHEWY
- ☐ OTHER............

NOTES

....
....
....

WOULD YOU TRY AGAIN?
- ☐ YES
- ☐ NO

OVERALL RATING
☆ ☆ ☆ ☆ ☆

Pizza Tasting Journal

DATE _____ PIZZERIA _____

NEIGHBOURHOOD _____

BEVERAGE PAIRING _____

TOPPINGS

- ☐ CHEESE
- ☐ MUSHROOMS
- ☐ GREEN PEPPER
- ☐ OTHER ....

- ☐ ONIONS
- ☐ BACON
- ☐ SAUSAGE

- ☐ PINEAPPLE
- ☐ TUNA
- ☐ BLACK OLIVES

CHEESE

- ☐ GREASY
- ☐ STINGY

- ☐ SMOKEY
- ☐ STINKY

- ☐ CREAMY
- ☐ SALTY

SAUCE

- ☐ SWEET
- ☐ TANGY

- ☐ THIN
- ☐ SAVORY

- ☐ SPICY
- ☐ CHUNKY

FRESHNESS ① ② ③ ④ ⑤   CRUST ① ② ③ ④ ⑤

CRUST

- ☐ BUTTERY
- ☐ CRISPY

- ☐ SPONGY
- ☐ BUBBLY

- ☐ CHEWY
- ☐ OTHER...........

NOTES

....

....

....

WOULD YOU TRY AGAIN?

☐ YES   ☐ NO

OVERALL RATING

☆ ☆ ☆ ☆ ☆

Pizza Tasting Journal

DATE _____ PIZZERIA _____

NEIGHBOURHOOD _____

BEVERAGE PAIRING _____

TOPPINGS

- ☐ CHEESE
- ☐ MUSHROOMS
- ☐ GREEN PEPPER
- ☐ OTHER ....

- ☐ ONIONS
- ☐ BACON
- ☐ SAUSAGE

- ☐ PINEAPPLE
- ☐ TUNA
- ☐ BLACK OLIVES

CHEESE

- ☐ GREASY
- ☐ STINGY

- ☐ SMOKEY
- ☐ STINKY

- ☐ CREAMY
- ☐ SALTY

SAUCE

- ☐ SWEET
- ☐ TANGY

- ☐ THIN
- ☐ SAVORY

- ☐ SPICY
- ☐ CHUNKY

FRESHNESS ① ② ③ ④ ⑤   CRUST ① ② ③ ④ ⑤

CRUST

- ☐ BUTTERY
- ☐ CRISPY

- ☐ SPONGY
- ☐ BUBBLY

- ☐ CHEWY
- ☐ OTHER...........

NOTES

....
....
....

WOULD YOU TRY AGAIN?
☐ YES   ☐ NO

OVERALL RATING
★ ★ ★ ★ ★

Pizza Tasting Journal

DATE _____ PIZZERIA _____

NEIGHBOURHOOD _____

BEVERAGE PAIRING _____

TOPPINGS

- [ ] CHEESE
- [ ] MUSHROOMS
- [ ] GREEN PEPPER
- [ ] OTHER ....
- [ ] ONIONS
- [ ] BACON
- [ ] SAUSAGE
- [ ] PINEAPPLE
- [ ] TUNA
- [ ] BLACK OLIVES

CHEESE

- [ ] GREASY
- [ ] STINGY
- [ ] SMOKEY
- [ ] STINKY
- [ ] CREAMY
- [ ] SALTY

SAUCE

- [ ] SWEET
- [ ] TANGY
- [ ] THIN
- [ ] SAVORY
- [ ] SPICY
- [ ] CHUNKY

FRESHNESS ① ② ③ ④ ⑤   CRUST ① ② ③ ④ ⑤

CRUST

- [ ] BUTTERY
- [ ] CRISPY
- [ ] SPONGY
- [ ] BUBBLY
- [ ] CHEWY
- [ ] OTHER...........

NOTES

....
....
....

WOULD YOU TRY AGAIN?

- [ ] YES
- [ ] NO

OVERALL RATING

★ ★ ★ ★ ★

Pizza Tasting Journal

DATE _____ PIZZERIA _____

NEIGHBOURHOOD _____

BEVERAGE PAIRING _____

TOPPINGS

- ☐ CHEESE
- ☐ MUSHROOMS
- ☐ GREEN PEPPER
- ☐ OTHER ....

- ☐ ONIONS
- ☐ BACON
- ☐ SAUSAGE

- ☐ PINEAPPLE
- ☐ TUNA
- ☐ BLACK OLIVES

CHEESE

- ☐ GREASY
- ☐ STINGY

- ☐ SMOKEY
- ☐ STINKY

- ☐ CREAMY
- ☐ SALTY

SAUCE

- ☐ SWEET
- ☐ TANGY

- ☐ THIN
- ☐ SAVORY

- ☐ SPICY
- ☐ CHUNKY

FRESHNESS ① ② ③ ④ ⑤   CRUST ① ② ③ ④ ⑤

CRUST

- ☐ BUTTERY
- ☐ CRISPY

- ☐ SPONGY
- ☐ BUBBLY

- ☐ CHEWY
- ☐ OTHER...........

NOTES

....
....
....

WOULD YOU TRY AGAIN?

☐ YES   ☐ NO

OVERALL RATING

★ ★ ★ ★ ★

Pizza Tasting Journal

DATE _____ PIZZERIA _____

NEIGHBOURHOOD _____

BEVERAGE PAIRING _____

TOPPINGS

- ☐ CHEESE
- ☐ MUSHROOMS
- ☐ GREEN PEPPER
- ☐ OTHER ....

- ☐ ONIONS
- ☐ BACON
- ☐ SAUSAGE

- ☐ PINEAPPLE
- ☐ TUNA
- ☐ BLACK OLIVES

CHEESE

- ☐ GREASY
- ☐ STINGY

- ☐ SMOKEY
- ☐ STINKY

- ☐ CREAMY
- ☐ SALTY

SAUCE

- ☐ SWEET
- ☐ TANGY

- ☐ THIN
- ☐ SAVORY

- ☐ SPICY
- ☐ CHUNKY

FRESHNESS ① ② ③ ④ ⑤   CRUST ① ② ③ ④ ⑤

CRUST

- ☐ BUTTERY
- ☐ CRISPY

- ☐ SPONGY
- ☐ BUBBLY

- ☐ CHEWY
- ☐ OTHER............

NOTES

....
....
....

WOULD YOU TRY AGAIN?
☐ YES   ☐ NO

OVERALL RATING
★ ★ ★ ★ ★

Pizza Tasting Journal

DATE _____ PIZZERIA _____

NEIGHBOURHOOD _____

BEVERAGE PAIRING _____

TOPPINGS

☐ CHEESE　　☐ ONIONS　　☐ PINEAPPLE
☐ MUSHROOMS　☐ BACON　　☐ TUNA
☐ GREEN PEPPER　☐ SAUSAGE　☐ BLACK OLIVES
☐ OTHER ....

CHEESE

☐ GREASY　　☐ SMOKEY　　☐ CREAMY
☐ STINGY　　☐ STINKY　　☐ SALTY

SAUCE

☐ SWEET　　☐ THIN　　☐ SPICY
☐ TANGY　　☐ SAVORY　　☐ CHUNKY

FRESHNESS ① ② ③ ④ ⑤　　CRUST ① ② ③ ④ ⑤

CRUST

☐ BUTTERY　　☐ SPONGY　　☐ CHEWY
☐ CRISPY　　☐ BUBBLY　　☐ OTHER...........

NOTES

....
....
....

WOULD YOU TRY AGAIN?　　**OVERALL RATING**
☐ YES　　☐ NO　　★ ★ ★ ★ ★

Pizza Tasting Journal

DATE _____ PIZZERIA _____

NEIGHBOURHOOD _____

BEVERAGE PAIRING _____

TOPPINGS

- [ ] CHEESE
- [ ] MUSHROOMS
- [ ] GREEN PEPPER
- [ ] OTHER ....

- [ ] ONIONS
- [ ] BACON
- [ ] SAUSAGE

- [ ] PINEAPPLE
- [ ] TUNA
- [ ] BLACK OLIVES

CHEESE

- [ ] GREASY
- [ ] STINGY

- [ ] SMOKEY
- [ ] STINKY

- [ ] CREAMY
- [ ] SALTY

SAUCE

- [ ] SWEET
- [ ] TANGY

- [ ] THIN
- [ ] SAVORY

- [ ] SPICY
- [ ] CHUNKY

FRESHNESS ① ② ③ ④ ⑤   CRUST ① ② ③ ④ ⑤

CRUST

- [ ] BUTTERY
- [ ] CRISPY

- [ ] SPONGY
- [ ] BUBBLY

- [ ] CHEWY
- [ ] OTHER...........

NOTES

....
....
....

WOULD YOU TRY AGAIN?
- [ ] YES
- [ ] NO

OVERALL RATING
☆ ☆ ☆ ☆ ☆

Pizza Tasting Journal

DATE _____   PIZZERIA _____

NEIGHBOURHOOD _____

BEVERAGE PAIRING _____

TOPPINGS

- ☐ CHEESE
- ☐ MUSHROOMS
- ☐ GREEN PEPPER
- ☐ OTHER ....

- ☐ ONIONS
- ☐ BACON
- ☐ SAUSAGE

- ☐ PINEAPPLE
- ☐ TUNA
- ☐ BLACK OLIVES

CHEESE

- ☐ GREASY
- ☐ STINGY

- ☐ SMOKEY
- ☐ STINKY

- ☐ CREAMY
- ☐ SALTY

SAUCE

- ☐ SWEET
- ☐ TANGY

- ☐ THIN
- ☐ SAVORY

- ☐ SPICY
- ☐ CHUNKY

FRESHNESS ① ② ③ ④ ⑤   CRUST ① ② ③ ④ ⑤

CRUST

- ☐ BUTTERY
- ☐ CRISPY

- ☐ SPONGY
- ☐ BUBBLY

- ☐ CHEWY
- ☐ OTHER...........

NOTES

....
....
....

WOULD YOU TRY AGAIN?
☐ YES   ☐ NO

OVERALL RATING
★ ★ ★ ★ ★

Pizza Tasting Journal

DATE _____ PIZZERIA _____

NEIGHBOURHOOD _____

BEVERAGE PAIRING _____

TOPPINGS

- ☐ CHEESE
- ☐ MUSHROOMS
- ☐ GREEN PEPPER
- ☐ OTHER ....

- ☐ ONIONS
- ☐ BACON
- ☐ SAUSAGE

- ☐ PINEAPPLE
- ☐ TUNA
- ☐ BLACK OLIVES

CHEESE

- ☐ GREASY
- ☐ STINGY

- ☐ SMOKEY
- ☐ STINKY

- ☐ CREAMY
- ☐ SALTY

SAUCE

- ☐ SWEET
- ☐ TANGY

- ☐ THIN
- ☐ SAVORY

- ☐ SPICY
- ☐ CHUNKY

FRESHNESS ① ② ③ ④ ⑤   CRUST ① ② ③ ④ ⑤

CRUST

- ☐ BUTTERY
- ☐ CRISPY

- ☐ SPONGY
- ☐ BUBBLY

- ☐ CHEWY
- ☐ OTHER............

NOTES

....
....
....

WOULD YOU TRY AGAIN?

☐ YES   ☐ NO

OVERALL RATING

☆ ☆ ☆ ☆ ☆

Pizza Tasting Journal

DATE   PIZZERIA

NEIGHBOURHOOD

BEVERAGE PAIRING

TOPPINGS

- ☐ CHEESE
- ☐ MUSHROOMS
- ☐ GREEN PEPPER
- ☐ OTHER ....

- ☐ ONIONS
- ☐ BACON
- ☐ SAUSAGE

- ☐ PINEAPPLE
- ☐ TUNA
- ☐ BLACK OLIVES

CHEESE

- ☐ GREASY
- ☐ STINGY

- ☐ SMOKEY
- ☐ STINKY

- ☐ CREAMY
- ☐ SALTY

SAUCE

- ☐ SWEET
- ☐ TANGY

- ☐ THIN
- ☐ SAVORY

- ☐ SPICY
- ☐ CHUNKY

FRESHNESS ① ② ③ ④ ⑤   CRUST ① ② ③ ④ ⑤

CRUST

- ☐ BUTTERY
- ☐ CRISPY

- ☐ SPONGY
- ☐ BUBBLY

- ☐ CHEWY
- ☐ OTHER...........

NOTES

....
....
....

WOULD YOU TRY AGAIN?

☐ YES   ☐ NO

OVERALL RATING

★ ★ ★ ★ ★

Pizza Tasting Journal

DATE _____ PIZZERIA _____

NEIGHBOURHOOD _____

BEVERAGE PAIRING _____

TOPPINGS

- ☐ CHEESE
- ☐ MUSHROOMS
- ☐ GREEN PEPPER
- ☐ OTHER ....

- ☐ ONIONS
- ☐ BACON
- ☐ SAUSAGE

- ☐ PINEAPPLE
- ☐ TUNA
- ☐ BLACK OLIVES

CHEESE

- ☐ GREASY
- ☐ STINGY

- ☐ SMOKEY
- ☐ STINKY

- ☐ CREAMY
- ☐ SALTY

SAUCE

- ☐ SWEET
- ☐ TANGY

- ☐ THIN
- ☐ SAVORY

- ☐ SPICY
- ☐ CHUNKY

FRESHNESS ① ② ③ ④ ⑤   CRUST ① ② ③ ④ ⑤

CRUST

- ☐ BUTTERY
- ☐ CRISPY

- ☐ SPONGY
- ☐ BUBBLY

- ☐ CHEWY
- ☐ OTHER............

NOTES

....
....
....

WOULD YOU TRY AGAIN?
☐ YES   ☐ NO

OVERALL RATING
☆ ☆ ☆ ☆ ☆

Pizza Tasting Journal

DATE _____ PIZZERIA _____

NEIGHBOURHOOD _____

BEVERAGE PAIRING _____

TOPPINGS

- ☐ CHEESE
- ☐ MUSHROOMS
- ☐ GREEN PEPPER
- ☐ OTHER ....
- ☐ ONIONS
- ☐ BACON
- ☐ SAUSAGE
- ☐ PINEAPPLE
- ☐ TUNA
- ☐ BLACK OLIVES

CHEESE

- ☐ GREASY
- ☐ STINGY
- ☐ SMOKEY
- ☐ STINKY
- ☐ CREAMY
- ☐ SALTY

SAUCE

- ☐ SWEET
- ☐ TANGY
- ☐ THIN
- ☐ SAVORY
- ☐ SPICY
- ☐ CHUNKY

FRESHNESS ① ② ③ ④ ⑤   CRUST ① ② ③ ④ ⑤

CRUST

- ☐ BUTTERY
- ☐ CRISPY
- ☐ SPONGY
- ☐ BUBBLY
- ☐ CHEWY
- ☐ OTHER............

NOTES

....
....
....

WOULD YOU TRY AGAIN?

☐ YES   ☐ NO

OVERALL RATING

☆ ☆ ☆ ☆ ☆

Pizza Tasting Journal

DATE _____ PIZZERIA _____

NEIGHBOURHOOD _____

BEVERAGE PAIRING _____

TOPPINGS

- [ ] CHEESE
- [ ] MUSHROOMS
- [ ] GREEN PEPPER
- [ ] OTHER ....

- [ ] ONIONS
- [ ] BACON
- [ ] SAUSAGE

- [ ] PINEAPPLE
- [ ] TUNA
- [ ] BLACK OLIVES

CHEESE

- [ ] GREASY
- [ ] STINGY

- [ ] SMOKEY
- [ ] STINKY

- [ ] CREAMY
- [ ] SALTY

SAUCE

- [ ] SWEET
- [ ] TANGY

- [ ] THIN
- [ ] SAVORY

- [ ] SPICY
- [ ] CHUNKY

FRESHNESS ① ② ③ ④ ⑤   CRUST ① ② ③ ④ ⑤

CRUST

- [ ] BUTTERY
- [ ] CRISPY

- [ ] SPONGY
- [ ] BUBBLY

- [ ] CHEWY
- [ ] OTHER...........

NOTES

....
....
....

WOULD YOU TRY AGAIN?
- [ ] YES
- [ ] NO

OVERALL RATING
☆ ☆ ☆ ☆ ☆

Pizza Tasting Journal

DATE _____ PIZZERIA _____

NEIGHBOURHOOD _____

BEVERAGE PAIRING _____

TOPPINGS

- ☐ CHEESE
- ☐ MUSHROOMS
- ☐ GREEN PEPPER
- ☐ OTHER ....

- ☐ ONIONS
- ☐ BACON
- ☐ SAUSAGE

- ☐ PINEAPPLE
- ☐ TUNA
- ☐ BLACK OLIVES

CHEESE

- ☐ GREASY
- ☐ STINGY

- ☐ SMOKEY
- ☐ STINKY

- ☐ CREAMY
- ☐ SALTY

SAUCE

- ☐ SWEET
- ☐ TANGY

- ☐ THIN
- ☐ SAVORY

- ☐ SPICY
- ☐ CHUNKY

FRESHNESS ① ② ③ ④ ⑤   CRUST ① ② ③ ④ ⑤

CRUST

- ☐ BUTTERY
- ☐ CRISPY

- ☐ SPONGY
- ☐ BUBBLY

- ☐ CHEWY
- ☐ OTHER...........

NOTES

....
....
....

WOULD YOU TRY AGAIN?
☐ YES   ☐ NO

OVERALL RATING
★ ★ ★ ★ ★

Pizza Tasting Journal

DATE _____ PIZZERIA _____

NEIGHBOURHOOD _____

BEVERAGE PAIRING _____

TOPPINGS

- ☐ CHEESE
- ☐ MUSHROOMS
- ☐ GREEN PEPPER
- ☐ OTHER ....

- ☐ ONIONS
- ☐ BACON
- ☐ SAUSAGE

- ☐ PINEAPPLE
- ☐ TUNA
- ☐ BLACK OLIVES

CHEESE

- ☐ GREASY
- ☐ STINGY

- ☐ SMOKEY
- ☐ STINKY

- ☐ CREAMY
- ☐ SALTY

SAUCE

- ☐ SWEET
- ☐ TANGY

- ☐ THIN
- ☐ SAVORY

- ☐ SPICY
- ☐ CHUNKY

FRESHNESS ① ② ③ ④ ⑤   CRUST ① ② ③ ④ ⑤

CRUST

- ☐ BUTTERY
- ☐ CRISPY

- ☐ SPONGY
- ☐ BUBBLY

- ☐ CHEWY
- ☐ OTHER............

NOTES

....
....
....

WOULD YOU TRY AGAIN?
☐ YES   ☐ NO

OVERALL RATING
★ ★ ★ ★ ★

Pizza Tasting Journal

DATE _____ PIZZERIA _____

NEIGHBOURHOOD _____

BEVERAGE PAIRING _____

TOPPINGS

- ☐ CHEESE
- ☐ MUSHROOMS
- ☐ GREEN PEPPER
- ☐ OTHER ....

- ☐ ONIONS
- ☐ BACON
- ☐ SAUSAGE

- ☐ PINEAPPLE
- ☐ TUNA
- ☐ BLACK OLIVES

CHEESE

- ☐ GREASY
- ☐ STINGY

- ☐ SMOKEY
- ☐ STINKY

- ☐ CREAMY
- ☐ SALTY

SAUCE

- ☐ SWEET
- ☐ TANGY

- ☐ THIN
- ☐ SAVORY

- ☐ SPICY
- ☐ CHUNKY

FRESHNESS ① ② ③ ④ ⑤   CRUST ① ② ③ ④ ⑤

CRUST

- ☐ BUTTERY
- ☐ CRISPY

- ☐ SPONGY
- ☐ BUBBLY

- ☐ CHEWY
- ☐ OTHER...........

NOTES

....
....
....

WOULD YOU TRY AGAIN?

☐ YES   ☐ NO

OVERALL RATING

★ ★ ★ ★ ★

Pizza Tasting Journal

DATE _____ PIZZERIA _____

NEIGHBOURHOOD _____

BEVERAGE PAIRING _____

TOPPINGS

☐ CHEESE   ☐ ONIONS   ☐ PINEAPPLE
☐ MUSHROOMS   ☐ BACON   ☐ TUNA
☐ GREEN PEPPER ☐ SAUSAGE   ☐ BLACK OLIVES
☐ OTHER ....

CHEESE

☐ GREASY   ☐ SMOKEY   ☐ CREAMY
☐ STINGY   ☐ STINKY   ☐ SALTY

SAUCE

☐ SWEET   ☐ THIN   ☐ SPICY
☐ TANGY   ☐ SAVORY   ☐ CHUNKY

FRESHNESS ① ② ③ ④ ⑤   CRUST ① ② ③ ④ ⑤

CRUST

☐ BUTTERY   ☐ SPONGY   ☐ CHEWY
☐ CRISPY   ☐ BUBBLY   ☐ OTHER...........

NOTES

....
....
....

WOULD YOU TRY AGAIN?   **OVERALL RATING**
☐ YES   ☐ NO   ☆ ☆ ☆ ☆ ☆

Pizza Tasting Journal

DATE _____ PIZZERIA _____

NEIGHBOURHOOD _____

BEVERAGE PAIRING _____

TOPPINGS

- [ ] CHEESE
- [ ] MUSHROOMS
- [ ] GREEN PEPPER
- [ ] OTHER ....

- [ ] ONIONS
- [ ] BACON
- [ ] SAUSAGE

- [ ] PINEAPPLE
- [ ] TUNA
- [ ] BLACK OLIVES

CHEESE

- [ ] GREASY
- [ ] STINGY

- [ ] SMOKEY
- [ ] STINKY

- [ ] CREAMY
- [ ] SALTY

SAUCE

- [ ] SWEET
- [ ] TANGY

- [ ] THIN
- [ ] SAVORY

- [ ] SPICY
- [ ] CHUNKY

FRESHNESS ① ② ③ ④ ⑤   CRUST ① ② ③ ④ ⑤

CRUST

- [ ] BUTTERY
- [ ] CRISPY

- [ ] SPONGY
- [ ] BUBBLY

- [ ] CHEWY
- [ ] OTHER...........

NOTES

....
....
....

WOULD YOU TRY AGAIN?
- [ ] YES   [ ] NO

OVERALL RATING
⭐ ⭐ ⭐ ⭐ ⭐

Pizza Tasting Journal

DATE .... PIZZERIA ....

NEIGHBOURHOOD ....

BEVERAGE PAIRING ....

TOPPINGS

- ☐ CHEESE
- ☐ MUSHROOMS
- ☐ GREEN PEPPER
- ☐ OTHER ....
- ☐ ONIONS
- ☐ BACON
- ☐ SAUSAGE
- ☐ PINEAPPLE
- ☐ TUNA
- ☐ BLACK OLIVES

CHEESE

- ☐ GREASY
- ☐ STINGY
- ☐ SMOKEY
- ☐ STINKY
- ☐ CREAMY
- ☐ SALTY

SAUCE

- ☐ SWEET
- ☐ TANGY
- ☐ THIN
- ☐ SAVORY
- ☐ SPICY
- ☐ CHUNKY

FRESHNESS ① ② ③ ④ ⑤   CRUST ① ② ③ ④ ⑤

CRUST

- ☐ BUTTERY
- ☐ CRISPY
- ☐ SPONGY
- ☐ BUBBLY
- ☐ CHEWY
- ☐ OTHER............

NOTES

....
....
....

WOULD YOU TRY AGAIN?

☐ YES   ☐ NO

OVERALL RATING

★ ★ ★ ★ ★

Pizza Tasting Journal

DATE _____ PIZZERIA _____

NEIGHBOURHOOD _____

BEVERAGE PAIRING _____

TOPPINGS

- ☐ CHEESE
- ☐ MUSHROOMS
- ☐ GREEN PEPPER
- ☐ OTHER ....
- ☐ ONIONS
- ☐ BACON
- ☐ SAUSAGE
- ☐ PINEAPPLE
- ☐ TUNA
- ☐ BLACK OLIVES

CHEESE

- ☐ GREASY
- ☐ STINGY
- ☐ SMOKEY
- ☐ STINKY
- ☐ CREAMY
- ☐ SALTY

SAUCE

- ☐ SWEET
- ☐ TANGY
- ☐ THIN
- ☐ SAVORY
- ☐ SPICY
- ☐ CHUNKY

FRESHNESS ① ② ③ ④ ⑤   CRUST ① ② ③ ④ ⑤

CRUST

- ☐ BUTTERY
- ☐ CRISPY
- ☐ SPONGY
- ☐ BUBBLY
- ☐ CHEWY
- ☐ OTHER...........

NOTES

....
....
....

WOULD YOU TRY AGAIN?
☐ YES   ☐ NO

OVERALL RATING
☆ ☆ ☆ ☆ ☆

Pizza Tasting Journal

DATE _____ PIZZERIA _____

NEIGHBOURHOOD _____

BEVERAGE PAIRING _____

TOPPINGS

- ☐ CHEESE
- ☐ MUSHROOMS
- ☐ GREEN PEPPER
- ☐ OTHER ....

- ☐ ONIONS
- ☐ BACON
- ☐ SAUSAGE

- ☐ PINEAPPLE
- ☐ TUNA
- ☐ BLACK OLIVES

CHEESE

- ☐ GREASY
- ☐ STINGY

- ☐ SMOKEY
- ☐ STINKY

- ☐ CREAMY
- ☐ SALTY

SAUCE

- ☐ SWEET
- ☐ TANGY

- ☐ THIN
- ☐ SAVORY

- ☐ SPICY
- ☐ CHUNKY

FRESHNESS ① ② ③ ④ ⑤   CRUST ① ② ③ ④ ⑤

CRUST

- ☐ BUTTERY
- ☐ CRISPY

- ☐ SPONGY
- ☐ BUBBLY

- ☐ CHEWY
- ☐ OTHER............

NOTES

....
....
....

WOULD YOU TRY AGAIN?
- ☐ YES
- ☐ NO

OVERALL RATING
☆ ☆ ☆ ☆ ☆

Pizza Tasting Journal

DATE _____   PIZZERIA _____

NEIGHBOURHOOD _____

BEVERAGE PAIRING _____

TOPPINGS

- ☐ CHEESE
- ☐ MUSHROOMS
- ☐ GREEN PEPPER
- ☐ OTHER ....

- ☐ ONIONS
- ☐ BACON
- ☐ SAUSAGE

- ☐ PINEAPPLE
- ☐ TUNA
- ☐ BLACK OLIVES

CHEESE

- ☐ GREASY
- ☐ STINGY

- ☐ SMOKEY
- ☐ STINKY

- ☐ CREAMY
- ☐ SALTY

SAUCE

- ☐ SWEET
- ☐ TANGY

- ☐ THIN
- ☐ SAVORY

- ☐ SPICY
- ☐ CHUNKY

FRESHNESS ① ② ③ ④ ⑤   CRUST ① ② ③ ④ ⑤

CRUST

- ☐ BUTTERY
- ☐ CRISPY

- ☐ SPONGY
- ☐ BUBBLY

- ☐ CHEWY
- ☐ OTHER...........

NOTES

....
....
....

WOULD YOU TRY AGAIN?
- ☐ YES   ☐ NO

OVERALL RATING
★ ★ ★ ★ ★

Pizza Tasting Journal

DATE _____ PIZZERIA _____

NEIGHBOURHOOD _____

BEVERAGE PAIRING _____

TOPPINGS

- [ ] CHEESE
- [ ] MUSHROOMS
- [ ] GREEN PEPPER
- [ ] OTHER ....

- [ ] ONIONS
- [ ] BACON
- [ ] SAUSAGE

- [ ] PINEAPPLE
- [ ] TUNA
- [ ] BLACK OLIVES

CHEESE

- [ ] GREASY
- [ ] STINGY

- [ ] SMOKEY
- [ ] STINKY

- [ ] CREAMY
- [ ] SALTY

SAUCE

- [ ] SWEET
- [ ] TANGY

- [ ] THIN
- [ ] SAVORY

- [ ] SPICY
- [ ] CHUNKY

FRESHNESS (1) (2) (3) (4) (5)   CRUST (1) (2) (3) (4) (5)

CRUST

- [ ] BUTTERY
- [ ] CRISPY

- [ ] SPONGY
- [ ] BUBBLY

- [ ] CHEWY
- [ ] OTHER............

NOTES

....
....
....

WOULD YOU TRY AGAIN?
- [ ] YES
- [ ] NO

OVERALL RATING
☆ ☆ ☆ ☆ ☆

Pizza Tasting Journal

DATE ⬜ PIZZERIA ⬜

NEIGHBOURHOOD ⬜

BEVERAGE PAIRING ⬜

TOPPINGS

☐ CHEESE ☐ ONIONS ☐ PINEAPPLE
☐ MUSHROOMS ☐ BACON ☐ TUNA
☐ GREEN PEPPER ☐ SAUSAGE ☐ BLACK OLIVES
☐ OTHER ....

CHEESE

☐ GREASY ☐ SMOKEY ☐ CREAMY
☐ STINGY ☐ STINKY ☐ SALTY

SAUCE

☐ SWEET ☐ THIN ☐ SPICY
☐ TANGY ☐ SAVORY ☐ CHUNKY

FRESHNESS ① ② ③ ④ ⑤   CRUST ① ② ③ ④ ⑤

CRUST

☐ BUTTERY ☐ SPONGY ☐ CHEWY
☐ CRISPY ☐ BUBBLY ☐ OTHER...........

NOTES

....
....
....

WOULD YOU TRY AGAIN?
☐ YES ☐ NO

OVERALL RATING
★ ★ ★ ★ ★

Pizza Tasting Journal

DATE _____ PIZZERIA _____

NEIGHBOURHOOD _____

BEVERAGE PAIRING _____

TOPPINGS

- ☐ CHEESE
- ☐ MUSHROOMS
- ☐ GREEN PEPPER
- ☐ OTHER ....
- ☐ ONIONS
- ☐ BACON
- ☐ SAUSAGE
- ☐ PINEAPPLE
- ☐ TUNA
- ☐ BLACK OLIVES

CHEESE

- ☐ GREASY
- ☐ STINGY
- ☐ SMOKEY
- ☐ STINKY
- ☐ CREAMY
- ☐ SALTY

SAUCE

- ☐ SWEET
- ☐ TANGY
- ☐ THIN
- ☐ SAVORY
- ☐ SPICY
- ☐ CHUNKY

FRESHNESS ① ② ③ ④ ⑤   CRUST ① ② ③ ④ ⑤

CRUST

- ☐ BUTTERY
- ☐ CRISPY
- ☐ SPONGY
- ☐ BUBBLY
- ☐ CHEWY
- ☐ OTHER...........

NOTES

....
....
....

WOULD YOU TRY AGAIN?
☐ YES ☐ NO

OVERALL RATING
☆ ☆ ☆ ☆ ☆

Pizza Tasting Journal

DATE _____ PIZZERIA _____

NEIGHBOURHOOD _____

BEVERAGE PAIRING _____

TOPPINGS

- ☐ CHEESE
- ☐ MUSHROOMS
- ☐ GREEN PEPPER
- ☐ OTHER ....

- ☐ ONIONS
- ☐ BACON
- ☐ SAUSAGE

- ☐ PINEAPPLE
- ☐ TUNA
- ☐ BLACK OLIVES

CHEESE

- ☐ GREASY
- ☐ STINGY

- ☐ SMOKEY
- ☐ STINKY

- ☐ CREAMY
- ☐ SALTY

SAUCE

- ☐ SWEET
- ☐ TANGY

- ☐ THIN
- ☐ SAVORY

- ☐ SPICY
- ☐ CHUNKY

FRESHNESS ① ② ③ ④ ⑤   CRUST ① ② ③ ④ ⑤

CRUST

- ☐ BUTTERY
- ☐ CRISPY

- ☐ SPONGY
- ☐ BUBBLY

- ☐ CHEWY
- ☐ OTHER...........

NOTES

....
....
....

WOULD YOU TRY AGAIN?
- ☐ YES   ☐ NO

OVERALL RATING
★ ★ ★ ★ ★

Pizza Tasting Journal

DATE _____ PIZZERIA _____

NEIGHBOURHOOD _____

BEVERAGE PAIRING _____

TOPPINGS

- ☐ CHEESE
- ☐ MUSHROOMS
- ☐ GREEN PEPPER
- ☐ OTHER ....

- ☐ ONIONS
- ☐ BACON
- ☐ SAUSAGE

- ☐ PINEAPPLE
- ☐ TUNA
- ☐ BLACK OLIVES

CHEESE

- ☐ GREASY
- ☐ STINGY

- ☐ SMOKEY
- ☐ STINKY

- ☐ CREAMY
- ☐ SALTY

SAUCE

- ☐ SWEET
- ☐ TANGY

- ☐ THIN
- ☐ SAVORY

- ☐ SPICY
- ☐ CHUNKY

FRESHNESS ① ② ③ ④ ⑤   CRUST ① ② ③ ④ ⑤

CRUST

- ☐ BUTTERY
- ☐ CRISPY

- ☐ SPONGY
- ☐ BUBBLY

- ☐ CHEWY
- ☐ OTHER...........

NOTES

....
....
....

WOULD YOU TRY AGAIN?
- ☐ YES
- ☐ NO

OVERALL RATING
★ ★ ★ ★ ★

Pizza Tasting Journal

DATE | PIZZERIA |

NEIGHBOURHOOD

BEVERAGE PAIRING

TOPPINGS

- [ ] CHEESE
- [ ] MUSHROOMS
- [ ] GREEN PEPPER
- [ ] OTHER ....

- [ ] ONIONS
- [ ] BACON
- [ ] SAUSAGE

- [ ] PINEAPPLE
- [ ] TUNA
- [ ] BLACK OLIVES

CHEESE

- [ ] GREASY
- [ ] STINGY

- [ ] SMOKEY
- [ ] STINKY

- [ ] CREAMY
- [ ] SALTY

SAUCE

- [ ] SWEET
- [ ] TANGY

- [ ] THIN
- [ ] SAVORY

- [ ] SPICY
- [ ] CHUNKY

FRESHNESS ① ② ③ ④ ⑤   CRUST ① ② ③ ④ ⑤

CRUST

- [ ] BUTTERY
- [ ] CRISPY

- [ ] SPONGY
- [ ] BUBBLY

- [ ] CHEWY
- [ ] OTHER............

NOTES

....
....
....

WOULD YOU TRY AGAIN?

- [ ] YES
- [ ] NO

OVERALL RATING

★ ★ ★ ★ ★

Pizza Tasting Journal

DATE _____   PIZZERIA _____

NEIGHBOURHOOD _____

BEVERAGE PAIRING _____

TOPPINGS

- [ ] CHEESE
- [ ] MUSHROOMS
- [ ] GREEN PEPPER
- [ ] OTHER ....
- [ ] ONIONS
- [ ] BACON
- [ ] SAUSAGE
- [ ] PINEAPPLE
- [ ] TUNA
- [ ] BLACK OLIVES

CHEESE

- [ ] GREASY
- [ ] STINGY
- [ ] SMOKEY
- [ ] STINKY
- [ ] CREAMY
- [ ] SALTY

SAUCE

- [ ] SWEET
- [ ] TANGY
- [ ] THIN
- [ ] SAVORY
- [ ] SPICY
- [ ] CHUNKY

FRESHNESS ① ② ③ ④ ⑤   CRUST ① ② ③ ④ ⑤

CRUST

- [ ] BUTTERY
- [ ] CRISPY
- [ ] SPONGY
- [ ] BUBBLY
- [ ] CHEWY
- [ ] OTHER............

NOTES

....
....
....

WOULD YOU TRY AGAIN?

- [ ] YES
- [ ] NO

OVERALL RATING

☆ ☆ ☆ ☆ ☆

Pizza Tasting Journal

DATE [   ] PIZZERIA [   ]

NEIGHBOURHOOD [   ]

BEVERAGE PAIRING [   ]

TOPPINGS

- ☐ CHEESE
- ☐ MUSHROOMS
- ☐ GREEN PEPPER
- ☐ OTHER ....

- ☐ ONIONS
- ☐ BACON
- ☐ SAUSAGE

- ☐ PINEAPPLE
- ☐ TUNA
- ☐ BLACK OLIVES

CHEESE

- ☐ GREASY
- ☐ STINGY

- ☐ SMOKEY
- ☐ STINKY

- ☐ CREAMY
- ☐ SALTY

SAUCE

- ☐ SWEET
- ☐ TANGY

- ☐ THIN
- ☐ SAVORY

- ☐ SPICY
- ☐ CHUNKY

FRESHNESS ① ② ③ ④ ⑤   CRUST ① ② ③ ④ ⑤

CRUST

- ☐ BUTTERY
- ☐ CRISPY

- ☐ SPONGY
- ☐ BUBBLY

- ☐ CHEWY
- ☐ OTHER...........

NOTES

....
....
....

WOULD YOU TRY AGAIN?

☐ YES   ☐ NO

OVERALL RATING

★ ★ ★ ★ ★

Pizza Tasting Journal

DATE _____ PIZZERIA _____

NEIGHBOURHOOD _____

BEVERAGE PAIRING _____

TOPPINGS

- ☐ CHEESE
- ☐ MUSHROOMS
- ☐ GREEN PEPPER
- ☐ OTHER ....

- ☐ ONIONS
- ☐ BACON
- ☐ SAUSAGE

- ☐ PINEAPPLE
- ☐ TUNA
- ☐ BLACK OLIVES

CHEESE

- ☐ GREASY
- ☐ STINGY

- ☐ SMOKEY
- ☐ STINKY

- ☐ CREAMY
- ☐ SALTY

SAUCE

- ☐ SWEET
- ☐ TANGY

- ☐ THIN
- ☐ SAVORY

- ☐ SPICY
- ☐ CHUNKY

FRESHNESS ① ② ③ ④ ⑤   CRUST ① ② ③ ④ ⑤

CRUST

- ☐ BUTTERY
- ☐ CRISPY

- ☐ SPONGY
- ☐ BUBBLY

- ☐ CHEWY
- ☐ OTHER............

NOTES

....
....
....

WOULD YOU TRY AGAIN?

☐ YES   ☐ NO

OVERALL RATING

☆ ☆ ☆ ☆ ☆

Pizza Tasting Journal

DATE _____ PIZZERIA _____

NEIGHBOURHOOD _____

BEVERAGE PAIRING _____

TOPPINGS

- ☐ CHEESE
- ☐ MUSHROOMS
- ☐ GREEN PEPPER
- ☐ OTHER ....
- ☐ ONIONS
- ☐ BACON
- ☐ SAUSAGE
- ☐ PINEAPPLE
- ☐ TUNA
- ☐ BLACK OLIVES

CHEESE

- ☐ GREASY
- ☐ STINGY
- ☐ SMOKEY
- ☐ STINKY
- ☐ CREAMY
- ☐ SALTY

SAUCE

- ☐ SWEET
- ☐ TANGY
- ☐ THIN
- ☐ SAVORY
- ☐ SPICY
- ☐ CHUNKY

FRESHNESS ① ② ③ ④ ⑤   CRUST ① ② ③ ④ ⑤

CRUST

- ☐ BUTTERY
- ☐ CRISPY
- ☐ SPONGY
- ☐ BUBBLY
- ☐ CHEWY
- ☐ OTHER...........

NOTES

....
....
....

WOULD YOU TRY AGAIN?
☐ YES   ☐ NO

OVERALL RATING
★ ★ ★ ★ ★

Pizza Tasting Journal

DATE _____   PIZZERIA _____

NEIGHBOURHOOD _____

BEVERAGE PAIRING _____

TOPPINGS

- ☐ CHEESE
- ☐ MUSHROOMS
- ☐ GREEN PEPPER
- ☐ OTHER ....

- ☐ ONIONS
- ☐ BACON
- ☐ SAUSAGE

- ☐ PINEAPPLE
- ☐ TUNA
- ☐ BLACK OLIVES

CHEESE

- ☐ GREASY
- ☐ STINGY

- ☐ SMOKEY
- ☐ STINKY

- ☐ CREAMY
- ☐ SALTY

SAUCE

- ☐ SWEET
- ☐ TANGY

- ☐ THIN
- ☐ SAVORY

- ☐ SPICY
- ☐ CHUNKY

FRESHNESS ① ② ③ ④ ⑤   CRUST ① ② ③ ④ ⑤

CRUST

- ☐ BUTTERY
- ☐ CRISPY

- ☐ SPONGY
- ☐ BUBBLY

- ☐ CHEWY
- ☐ OTHER............

NOTES

....
....
....

WOULD YOU TRY AGAIN?
- ☐ YES
- ☐ NO

OVERALL RATING
★ ★ ★ ★ ★

Pizza Tasting Journal

DATE _____ PIZZERIA _____

NEIGHBOURHOOD _____

BEVERAGE PAIRING _____

TOPPINGS

- ☐ CHEESE
- ☐ MUSHROOMS
- ☐ GREEN PEPPER
- ☐ OTHER ....

- ☐ ONIONS
- ☐ BACON
- ☐ SAUSAGE

- ☐ PINEAPPLE
- ☐ TUNA
- ☐ BLACK OLIVES

CHEESE

- ☐ GREASY
- ☐ STINGY

- ☐ SMOKEY
- ☐ STINKY

- ☐ CREAMY
- ☐ SALTY

SAUCE

- ☐ SWEET
- ☐ TANGY

- ☐ THIN
- ☐ SAVORY

- ☐ SPICY
- ☐ CHUNKY

FRESHNESS ① ② ③ ④ ⑤   CRUST ① ② ③ ④ ⑤

CRUST

- ☐ BUTTERY
- ☐ CRISPY

- ☐ SPONGY
- ☐ BUBBLY

- ☐ CHEWY
- ☐ OTHER............

NOTES

....
....
....

WOULD YOU TRY AGAIN?
☐ YES ☐ NO

OVERALL RATING
★ ★ ★ ★ ★

Pizza Tasting Journal

DATE .... PIZZERIA ....

NEIGHBOURHOOD ....

BEVERAGE PAIRING ....

TOPPINGS

☐ CHEESE   ☐ ONIONS   ☐ PINEAPPLE

☐ MUSHROOMS   ☐ BACON   ☐ TUNA

☐ GREEN PEPPER   ☐ SAUSAGE   ☐ BLACK OLIVES

☐ OTHER ....

CHEESE

☐ GREASY   ☐ SMOKEY   ☐ CREAMY

☐ STINGY   ☐ STINKY   ☐ SALTY

SAUCE

☐ SWEET   ☐ THIN   ☐ SPICY

☐ TANGY   ☐ SAVORY   ☐ CHUNKY

FRESHNESS ① ② ③ ④ ⑤   CRUST ① ② ③ ④ ⑤

CRUST

☐ BUTTERY   ☐ SPONGY   ☐ CHEWY

☐ CRISPY   ☐ BUBBLY   ☐ OTHER............

NOTES

....

....

....

WOULD YOU TRY AGAIN?

☐ YES   ☐ NO

OVERALL RATING

☆ ☆ ☆ ☆ ☆

Pizza Tasting Journal

DATE _____ PIZZERIA _____

NEIGHBOURHOOD _____

BEVERAGE PAIRING _____

TOPPINGS

- ☐ CHEESE
- ☐ MUSHROOMS
- ☐ GREEN PEPPER
- ☐ OTHER ....

- ☐ ONIONS
- ☐ BACON
- ☐ SAUSAGE

- ☐ PINEAPPLE
- ☐ TUNA
- ☐ BLACK OLIVES

CHEESE

- ☐ GREASY
- ☐ STINGY

- ☐ SMOKEY
- ☐ STINKY

- ☐ CREAMY
- ☐ SALTY

SAUCE

- ☐ SWEET
- ☐ TANGY

- ☐ THIN
- ☐ SAVORY

- ☐ SPICY
- ☐ CHUNKY

FRESHNESS ① ② ③ ④ ⑤   CRUST ① ② ③ ④ ⑤

CRUST

- ☐ BUTTERY
- ☐ CRISPY

- ☐ SPONGY
- ☐ BUBBLY

- ☐ CHEWY
- ☐ OTHER...........

NOTES

....
....
....

WOULD YOU TRY AGAIN?
☐ YES ☐ NO

OVERALL RATING
★ ★ ★ ★ ★

Pizza Tasting Journal

DATE _____ PIZZERIA _____

NEIGHBOURHOOD _____

BEVERAGE PAIRING _____

TOPPINGS

- ☐ CHEESE
- ☐ MUSHROOMS
- ☐ GREEN PEPPER
- ☐ OTHER ....

- ☐ ONIONS
- ☐ BACON
- ☐ SAUSAGE

- ☐ PINEAPPLE
- ☐ TUNA
- ☐ BLACK OLIVES

CHEESE

- ☐ GREASY
- ☐ STINGY

- ☐ SMOKEY
- ☐ STINKY

- ☐ CREAMY
- ☐ SALTY

SAUCE

- ☐ SWEET
- ☐ TANGY

- ☐ THIN
- ☐ SAVORY

- ☐ SPICY
- ☐ CHUNKY

FRESHNESS ① ② ③ ④ ⑤   CRUST ① ② ③ ④ ⑤

CRUST

- ☐ BUTTERY
- ☐ CRISPY

- ☐ SPONGY
- ☐ BUBBLY

- ☐ CHEWY
- ☐ OTHER...........

NOTES

....
....
....

WOULD YOU TRY AGAIN?

☐ YES   ☐ NO

OVERALL RATING

★ ★ ★ ★ ★

Pizza Tasting Journal

DATE _____ PIZZERIA _____

NEIGHBOURHOOD _____

BEVERAGE PAIRING _____

TOPPINGS

- [ ] CHEESE
- [ ] MUSHROOMS
- [ ] GREEN PEPPER
- [ ] OTHER ....

- [ ] ONIONS
- [ ] BACON
- [ ] SAUSAGE

- [ ] PINEAPPLE
- [ ] TUNA
- [ ] BLACK OLIVES

CHEESE

- [ ] GREASY
- [ ] STINGY

- [ ] SMOKEY
- [ ] STINKY

- [ ] CREAMY
- [ ] SALTY

SAUCE

- [ ] SWEET
- [ ] TANGY

- [ ] THIN
- [ ] SAVORY

- [ ] SPICY
- [ ] CHUNKY

FRESHNESS ① ② ③ ④ ⑤   CRUST ① ② ③ ④ ⑤

CRUST

- [ ] BUTTERY
- [ ] CRISPY

- [ ] SPONGY
- [ ] BUBBLY

- [ ] CHEWY
- [ ] OTHER...........

NOTES

....
....
....

WOULD YOU TRY AGAIN?

- [ ] YES   - [ ] NO

OVERALL RATING

★ ★ ★ ★ ★

Pizza Tasting Journal

DATE _____ PIZZERIA _____

NEIGHBOURHOOD _____

BEVERAGE PAIRING _____

TOPPINGS

- [ ] CHEESE
- [ ] MUSHROOMS
- [ ] GREEN PEPPER
- [ ] OTHER ....

- [ ] ONIONS
- [ ] BACON
- [ ] SAUSAGE

- [ ] PINEAPPLE
- [ ] TUNA
- [ ] BLACK OLIVES

CHEESE

- [ ] GREASY
- [ ] STINGY

- [ ] SMOKEY
- [ ] STINKY

- [ ] CREAMY
- [ ] SALTY

SAUCE

- [ ] SWEET
- [ ] TANGY

- [ ] THIN
- [ ] SAVORY

- [ ] SPICY
- [ ] CHUNKY

FRESHNESS (1) (2) (3) (4) (5)   CRUST (1) (2) (3) (4) (5)

CRUST

- [ ] BUTTERY
- [ ] CRISPY

- [ ] SPONGY
- [ ] BUBBLY

- [ ] CHEWY
- [ ] OTHER...........

NOTES

....
....
....

WOULD YOU TRY AGAIN?
- [ ] YES   - [ ] NO

OVERALL RATING
☆ ☆ ☆ ☆ ☆

Pizza Tasting Journal

DATE   PIZZERIA

NEIGHBOURHOOD

BEVERAGE PAIRING

TOPPINGS

- ☐ CHEESE
- ☐ MUSHROOMS
- ☐ GREEN PEPPER
- ☐ OTHER ....
- ☐ ONIONS
- ☐ BACON
- ☐ SAUSAGE
- ☐ PINEAPPLE
- ☐ TUNA
- ☐ BLACK OLIVES

CHEESE

- ☐ GREASY
- ☐ STINGY
- ☐ SMOKEY
- ☐ STINKY
- ☐ CREAMY
- ☐ SALTY

SAUCE

- ☐ SWEET
- ☐ TANGY
- ☐ THIN
- ☐ SAVORY
- ☐ SPICY
- ☐ CHUNKY

FRESHNESS ① ② ③ ④ ⑤   CRUST ① ② ③ ④ ⑤

CRUST

- ☐ BUTTERY
- ☐ CRISPY
- ☐ SPONGY
- ☐ BUBBLY
- ☐ CHEWY
- ☐ OTHER...........

NOTES

....
....
....

WOULD YOU TRY AGAIN?

☐ YES   ☐ NO

OVERALL RATING

★ ★ ★ ★ ★

Pizza Tasting Journal

DATE _____ PIZZERIA _____

NEIGHBOURHOOD _____

BEVERAGE PAIRING _____

TOPPINGS

- ☐ CHEESE
- ☐ MUSHROOMS
- ☐ GREEN PEPPER
- ☐ OTHER ....

- ☐ ONIONS
- ☐ BACON
- ☐ SAUSAGE

- ☐ PINEAPPLE
- ☐ TUNA
- ☐ BLACK OLIVES

CHEESE

- ☐ GREASY
- ☐ STINGY

- ☐ SMOKEY
- ☐ STINKY

- ☐ CREAMY
- ☐ SALTY

SAUCE

- ☐ SWEET
- ☐ TANGY

- ☐ THIN
- ☐ SAVORY

- ☐ SPICY
- ☐ CHUNKY

FRESHNESS ① ② ③ ④ ⑤   CRUST ① ② ③ ④ ⑤

CRUST

- ☐ BUTTERY
- ☐ CRISPY

- ☐ SPONGY
- ☐ BUBBLY

- ☐ CHEWY
- ☐ OTHER...........

NOTES

....
....
....

WOULD YOU TRY AGAIN?
☐ YES   ☐ NO

OVERALL RATING
★ ★ ★ ★ ★

Pizza Tasting Journal

DATE _____ PIZZERIA _____

NEIGHBOURHOOD _____

BEVERAGE PAIRING _____

TOPPINGS

- ☐ CHEESE
- ☐ MUSHROOMS
- ☐ GREEN PEPPER
- ☐ OTHER ....

- ☐ ONIONS
- ☐ BACON
- ☐ SAUSAGE

- ☐ PINEAPPLE
- ☐ TUNA
- ☐ BLACK OLIVES

CHEESE

- ☐ GREASY
- ☐ STINGY

- ☐ SMOKEY
- ☐ STINKY

- ☐ CREAMY
- ☐ SALTY

SAUCE

- ☐ SWEET
- ☐ TANGY

- ☐ THIN
- ☐ SAVORY

- ☐ SPICY
- ☐ CHUNKY

FRESHNESS ① ② ③ ④ ⑤   CRUST ① ② ③ ④ ⑤

CRUST

- ☐ BUTTERY
- ☐ CRISPY

- ☐ SPONGY
- ☐ BUBBLY

- ☐ CHEWY
- ☐ OTHER...........

NOTES

....
....
....

WOULD YOU TRY AGAIN?
☐ YES   ☐ NO

OVERALL RATING
★ ★ ★ ★ ★

Pizza Tasting Journal

DATE _____ PIZZERIA _____

NEIGHBOURHOOD _____

BEVERAGE PAIRING _____

TOPPINGS

- ☐ CHEESE
- ☐ MUSHROOMS
- ☐ GREEN PEPPER
- ☐ OTHER ....

- ☐ ONIONS
- ☐ BACON
- ☐ SAUSAGE

- ☐ PINEAPPLE
- ☐ TUNA
- ☐ BLACK OLIVES

CHEESE

- ☐ GREASY
- ☐ STINGY

- ☐ SMOKEY
- ☐ STINKY

- ☐ CREAMY
- ☐ SALTY

SAUCE

- ☐ SWEET
- ☐ TANGY

- ☐ THIN
- ☐ SAVORY

- ☐ SPICY
- ☐ CHUNKY

FRESHNESS ① ② ③ ④ ⑤   CRUST ① ② ③ ④ ⑤

CRUST

- ☐ BUTTERY
- ☐ CRISPY

- ☐ SPONGY
- ☐ BUBBLY

- ☐ CHEWY
- ☐ OTHER............

NOTES

....
....
....

WOULD YOU TRY AGAIN?
☐ YES   ☐ NO

OVERALL RATING
☆ ☆ ☆ ☆ ☆

Pizza Tasting Journal

DATE _____   PIZZERIA _____

NEIGHBOURHOOD _____

BEVERAGE PAIRING _____

TOPPINGS

- ☐ CHEESE
- ☐ MUSHROOMS
- ☐ GREEN PEPPER
- ☐ OTHER ....

- ☐ ONIONS
- ☐ BACON
- ☐ SAUSAGE

- ☐ PINEAPPLE
- ☐ TUNA
- ☐ BLACK OLIVES

CHEESE

- ☐ GREASY
- ☐ STINGY

- ☐ SMOKEY
- ☐ STINKY

- ☐ CREAMY
- ☐ SALTY

SAUCE

- ☐ SWEET
- ☐ TANGY

- ☐ THIN
- ☐ SAVORY

- ☐ SPICY
- ☐ CHUNKY

FRESHNESS ① ② ③ ④ ⑤   CRUST ① ② ③ ④ ⑤

CRUST

- ☐ BUTTERY
- ☐ CRISPY

- ☐ SPONGY
- ☐ BUBBLY

- ☐ CHEWY
- ☐ OTHER...........

NOTES

....
....
....

WOULD YOU TRY AGAIN?

☐ YES   ☐ NO

OVERALL RATING

★ ★ ★ ★ ★

Pizza Tasting Journal

DATE _____   PIZZERIA _____

NEIGHBOURHOOD _____

BEVERAGE PAIRING _____

TOPPINGS

- ☐ CHEESE
- ☐ MUSHROOMS
- ☐ GREEN PEPPER
- ☐ OTHER ....

- ☐ ONIONS
- ☐ BACON
- ☐ SAUSAGE

- ☐ PINEAPPLE
- ☐ TUNA
- ☐ BLACK OLIVES

CHEESE

- ☐ GREASY
- ☐ STINGY

- ☐ SMOKEY
- ☐ STINKY

- ☐ CREAMY
- ☐ SALTY

SAUCE

- ☐ SWEET
- ☐ TANGY

- ☐ THIN
- ☐ SAVORY

- ☐ SPICY
- ☐ CHUNKY

FRESHNESS ① ② ③ ④ ⑤   CRUST ① ② ③ ④ ⑤

CRUST

- ☐ BUTTERY
- ☐ CRISPY

- ☐ SPONGY
- ☐ BUBBLY

- ☐ CHEWY
- ☐ OTHER...........

NOTES

....
....
....

WOULD YOU TRY AGAIN?
- ☐ YES   ☐ NO

OVERALL RATING
☆ ☆ ☆ ☆ ☆

Pizza Tasting Journal

DATE _____ PIZZERIA _____

NEIGHBOURHOOD _____

BEVERAGE PAIRING _____

TOPPINGS

- ☐ CHEESE
- ☐ MUSHROOMS
- ☐ GREEN PEPPER
- ☐ OTHER ....

- ☐ ONIONS
- ☐ BACON
- ☐ SAUSAGE

- ☐ PINEAPPLE
- ☐ TUNA
- ☐ BLACK OLIVES

CHEESE

- ☐ GREASY
- ☐ STINGY

- ☐ SMOKEY
- ☐ STINKY

- ☐ CREAMY
- ☐ SALTY

SAUCE

- ☐ SWEET
- ☐ TANGY

- ☐ THIN
- ☐ SAVORY

- ☐ SPICY
- ☐ CHUNKY

FRESHNESS ① ② ③ ④ ⑤   CRUST ① ② ③ ④ ⑤

CRUST

- ☐ BUTTERY
- ☐ CRISPY

- ☐ SPONGY
- ☐ BUBBLY

- ☐ CHEWY
- ☐ OTHER...........

NOTES

....
....
....

WOULD YOU TRY AGAIN?
☐ YES   ☐ NO

OVERALL RATING
★ ★ ★ ★ ★

Pizza Tasting Journal

DATE _____ PIZZERIA _____

NEIGHBOURHOOD _____

BEVERAGE PAIRING _____

TOPPINGS

- ☐ CHEESE
- ☐ MUSHROOMS
- ☐ GREEN PEPPER
- ☐ OTHER ....
- ☐ ONIONS
- ☐ BACON
- ☐ SAUSAGE
- ☐ PINEAPPLE
- ☐ TUNA
- ☐ BLACK OLIVES

CHEESE

- ☐ GREASY
- ☐ STINGY
- ☐ SMOKEY
- ☐ STINKY
- ☐ CREAMY
- ☐ SALTY

SAUCE

- ☐ SWEET
- ☐ TANGY
- ☐ THIN
- ☐ SAVORY
- ☐ SPICY
- ☐ CHUNKY

FRESHNESS ① ② ③ ④ ⑤   CRUST ① ② ③ ④ ⑤

CRUST

- ☐ BUTTERY
- ☐ CRISPY
- ☐ SPONGY
- ☐ BUBBLY
- ☐ CHEWY
- ☐ OTHER...........

NOTES

....
....
....

WOULD YOU TRY AGAIN?

☐ YES   ☐ NO

OVERALL RATING

☆ ☆ ☆ ☆ ☆

Pizza Tasting Journal

DATE _____ PIZZERIA _____

NEIGHBOURHOOD _____

BEVERAGE PAIRING _____

TOPPINGS

- ☐ CHEESE
- ☐ MUSHROOMS
- ☐ GREEN PEPPER
- ☐ OTHER ....
- ☐ ONIONS
- ☐ BACON
- ☐ SAUSAGE
- ☐ PINEAPPLE
- ☐ TUNA
- ☐ BLACK OLIVES

CHEESE

- ☐ GREASY
- ☐ STINGY
- ☐ SMOKEY
- ☐ STINKY
- ☐ CREAMY
- ☐ SALTY

SAUCE

- ☐ SWEET
- ☐ TANGY
- ☐ THIN
- ☐ SAVORY
- ☐ SPICY
- ☐ CHUNKY

FRESHNESS ① ② ③ ④ ⑤   CRUST ① ② ③ ④ ⑤

CRUST

- ☐ BUTTERY
- ☐ CRISPY
- ☐ SPONGY
- ☐ BUBBLY
- ☐ CHEWY
- ☐ OTHER...........

NOTES

....
....
....

WOULD YOU TRY AGAIN?
☐ YES   ☐ NO

OVERALL RATING
☆ ☆ ☆ ☆ ☆

Pizza Tasting Journal

DATE _____ PIZZERIA _____

NEIGHBOURHOOD _____

BEVERAGE PAIRING _____

TOPPINGS

- ☐ CHEESE
- ☐ MUSHROOMS
- ☐ GREEN PEPPER
- ☐ OTHER ....

- ☐ ONIONS
- ☐ BACON
- ☐ SAUSAGE

- ☐ PINEAPPLE
- ☐ TUNA
- ☐ BLACK OLIVES

CHEESE

- ☐ GREASY
- ☐ STINGY

- ☐ SMOKEY
- ☐ STINKY

- ☐ CREAMY
- ☐ SALTY

SAUCE

- ☐ SWEET
- ☐ TANGY

- ☐ THIN
- ☐ SAVORY

- ☐ SPICY
- ☐ CHUNKY

FRESHNESS ① ② ③ ④ ⑤   CRUST ① ② ③ ④ ⑤

CRUST

- ☐ BUTTERY
- ☐ CRISPY

- ☐ SPONGY
- ☐ BUBBLY

- ☐ CHEWY
- ☐ OTHER............

NOTES

....
....
....

WOULD YOU TRY AGAIN?
- ☐ YES
- ☐ NO

OVERALL RATING
★ ★ ★ ★ ★

Pizza Tasting Journal

DATE _____   PIZZERIA _____

NEIGHBOURHOOD _____

BEVERAGE PAIRING _____

TOPPINGS

- ☐ CHEESE
- ☐ MUSHROOMS
- ☐ GREEN PEPPER
- ☐ OTHER ....
- ☐ ONIONS
- ☐ BACON
- ☐ SAUSAGE
- ☐ PINEAPPLE
- ☐ TUNA
- ☐ BLACK OLIVES

CHEESE

- ☐ GREASY
- ☐ STINGY
- ☐ SMOKEY
- ☐ STINKY
- ☐ CREAMY
- ☐ SALTY

SAUCE

- ☐ SWEET
- ☐ TANGY
- ☐ THIN
- ☐ SAVORY
- ☐ SPICY
- ☐ CHUNKY

FRESHNESS ① ② ③ ④ ⑤   CRUST ① ② ③ ④ ⑤

CRUST

- ☐ BUTTERY
- ☐ CRISPY
- ☐ SPONGY
- ☐ BUBBLY
- ☐ CHEWY
- ☐ OTHER............

NOTES

....
....
....

WOULD YOU TRY AGAIN?

☐ YES   ☐ NO

OVERALL RATING

★ ★ ★ ★ ★

Pizza Tasting Journal

DATE .... PIZZERIA ....

NEIGHBOURHOOD ....

BEVERAGE PAIRING ....

TOPPINGS

- ☐ CHEESE
- ☐ MUSHROOMS
- ☐ GREEN PEPPER
- ☐ OTHER ....

- ☐ ONIONS
- ☐ BACON
- ☐ SAUSAGE

- ☐ PINEAPPLE
- ☐ TUNA
- ☐ BLACK OLIVES

CHEESE

- ☐ GREASY
- ☐ STINGY

- ☐ SMOKEY
- ☐ STINKY

- ☐ CREAMY
- ☐ SALTY

SAUCE

- ☐ SWEET
- ☐ TANGY

- ☐ THIN
- ☐ SAVORY

- ☐ SPICY
- ☐ CHUNKY

FRESHNESS ① ② ③ ④ ⑤   CRUST ① ② ③ ④ ⑤

CRUST

- ☐ BUTTERY
- ☐ CRISPY

- ☐ SPONGY
- ☐ BUBBLY

- ☐ CHEWY
- ☐ OTHER............

NOTES

....
....
....

WOULD YOU TRY AGAIN?

☐ YES   ☐ NO

OVERALL RATING

☆ ☆ ☆ ☆ ☆

Pizza Tasting Journal

DATE _____   PIZZERIA _____

NEIGHBOURHOOD _____

BEVERAGE PAIRING _____

TOPPINGS

- ☐ CHEESE
- ☐ MUSHROOMS
- ☐ GREEN PEPPER
- ☐ OTHER ....

- ☐ ONIONS
- ☐ BACON
- ☐ SAUSAGE

- ☐ PINEAPPLE
- ☐ TUNA
- ☐ BLACK OLIVES

CHEESE

- ☐ GREASY
- ☐ STINGY

- ☐ SMOKEY
- ☐ STINKY

- ☐ CREAMY
- ☐ SALTY

SAUCE

- ☐ SWEET
- ☐ TANGY

- ☐ THIN
- ☐ SAVORY

- ☐ SPICY
- ☐ CHUNKY

FRESHNESS ① ② ③ ④ ⑤   CRUST ① ② ③ ④ ⑤

CRUST

- ☐ BUTTERY
- ☐ CRISPY

- ☐ SPONGY
- ☐ BUBBLY

- ☐ CHEWY
- ☐ OTHER............

NOTES

....
....
....

WOULD YOU TRY AGAIN?

☐ YES   ☐ NO

OVERALL RATING

★ ★ ★ ★ ★

Pizza Tasting Journal

DATE _____ PIZZERIA _____

NEIGHBOURHOOD _____

BEVERAGE PAIRING _____

TOPPINGS

- ☐ CHEESE
- ☐ MUSHROOMS
- ☐ GREEN PEPPER
- ☐ OTHER ....
- ☐ ONIONS
- ☐ BACON
- ☐ SAUSAGE
- ☐ PINEAPPLE
- ☐ TUNA
- ☐ BLACK OLIVES

CHEESE

- ☐ GREASY
- ☐ STINGY
- ☐ SMOKEY
- ☐ STINKY
- ☐ CREAMY
- ☐ SALTY

SAUCE

- ☐ SWEET
- ☐ TANGY
- ☐ THIN
- ☐ SAVORY
- ☐ SPICY
- ☐ CHUNKY

FRESHNESS ① ② ③ ④ ⑤   CRUST ① ② ③ ④ ⑤

CRUST

- ☐ BUTTERY
- ☐ CRISPY
- ☐ SPONGY
- ☐ BUBBLY
- ☐ CHEWY
- ☐ OTHER............

NOTES

....
....
....

WOULD YOU TRY AGAIN?
   ☐ YES   ☐ NO

OVERALL RATING
☆ ☆ ☆ ☆ ☆

Pizza Tasting Journal

DATE _____ PIZZERIA _____

NEIGHBOURHOOD _____

BEVERAGE PAIRING _____

TOPPINGS

☐ CHEESE ☐ ONIONS ☐ PINEAPPLE
☐ MUSHROOMS ☐ BACON ☐ TUNA
☐ GREEN PEPPER ☐ SAUSAGE ☐ BLACK OLIVES
☐ OTHER ....

CHEESE

☐ GREASY ☐ SMOKEY ☐ CREAMY
☐ STINGY ☐ STINKY ☐ SALTY

SAUCE

☐ SWEET ☐ THIN ☐ SPICY
☐ TANGY ☐ SAVORY ☐ CHUNKY

FRESHNESS ① ② ③ ④ ⑤   CRUST ① ② ③ ④ ⑤

CRUST

☐ BUTTERY ☐ SPONGY ☐ CHEWY
☐ CRISPY ☐ BUBBLY ☐ OTHER............

NOTES

....
....
....

WOULD YOU TRY AGAIN?
☐ YES ☐ NO

OVERALL RATING
★ ★ ★ ★ ★

Printed in Great Britain
by Amazon

22678818R00062